Casteism in India

Is it the Scourge of Hinduism or the Perversion of a Legitimate Vedic System Known as Varnashrama

By
Stephen Knapp

Cover photo: A temple at twilight in the area of Mayapur, India, by Stephen Knapp.

Published by
The World Relief Network
Detroit, Michigan, USA

ISBN-10: 1530963842
ISBN-13: 978-1530963843

You can find out more about
Stephen Knapp
and his books, free ebooks, research,
and numerous articles and photos,
along with many other spiritual resources at:
http://www.stephen-knapp.com or
http://stephenknapp.info
http://stephenknapp.wordpress.com

Other books by the author:

1. The Secret Teachings of the Vedas: The Eastern Answers to the Mysteries of Life
2. The Universal Path to Enlightenment
3. The Vedic Prophecies: A New Look into the Future
4. How the Universe was Created and Our Purpose In It
5. Toward World Peace: Seeing the Unity Between Us All
6. Facing Death: Welcoming the Afterlife
7. The Key to Real Happiness
8. Proof of Vedic Culture's Global Existence
9. The Heart of Hinduism: The Eastern Path to Freedom, Enlightenment and Illumination
10. The Power of the Dharma: An Introduction to Hinduism and Vedic Culture
11. Vedic Culture: The Difference it can Make in Your Life
12. Reincarnation & Karma: How They Really Affect Us
13. The Eleventh Commandment: The Next Step for Social Spiritual Development
14. Seeing Spiritual India: A Guide to Temples, Holy Sites, Festivals and Traditions
15. Crimes Against India: And the Need to Protect its Ancient Vedic Tradition
16. Destined for Infinity, a spiritual adventure in the Himalayas
17. Yoga and Meditation: Their Real Purpose and How to Get Started
18. Avatars, Gods and Goddesses of Vedic Culture: Understanding the Characteristics, Powers and Positions of the Hindu Divinities
19. The Soul: Understanding Our Real Identity
20. Prayers, Mantras and Gayatris: A Collection for Insights, Protection, Spiritual Growth, and Many Other Blessings
21. Krishna Deities and Their Miracles: How the Images of Lord Krishna Interact with Their Devotees
22. Defending Vedic Dharma: Tackling the Issues to Make a Difference.
23. Advancements of Ancient India's Vedic Culture.
24. Spreading Vedic Traditions Through Temples.
25. The Bhakti-yoga Handbook: A Guide to Beginning the Essentials of Devotional Yoga.
26. Lord Krishna and His Essential Teachings.
27. Mysteries of the Ancient Vedic Empire.

CONTENTS

Contents

Understanding * Knowledge * Sacrifices * Austerities *
Charity * Foods * Happiness * Where the Modes Take Us
* Becoming Free From the Modes

CHAPTER ONE

The Purpose of the Vedic System of Varnashrama

Casteism in India has gotten a lot of criticism, and rightly so. The way casteism is at present should not even exist. We should throw it out. Casteism as we find it today is now nothing more than a misrepresentation and misinterpretation of a legitimate and progressive Vedic system known as varnashrama. What that is we will explain shortly. However, we need to know the difference between the two, then get rid of present-day casteism to again utilize the genuine and liberal form of social organization, known as varnashrama.

WHAT CASTEISM IS TODAY

The casteism that we find today is the materialistic form of designation that has become a way of oppressing the lower social orders of people. It says that if you are born in a family of a certain classification, then you are of the same class with little possibility of changing. In casteism, birth is now the major factor in determining one's social standing. It dictates that your social order, occupational potential and characteristics are the same as your parents, which is a label that may have been placed on a family hundreds of years ago.

In the Vedic system, there were four basic

classifications. There were the Brahmanas (priests and intellectuals, those who practiced and preserved the Vedic rituals and processes of spiritual realization), the Kshatriyas (warriors, military, government administrators), Vaishyas (the merchants, bankers, farmers, etc.), and the Shudras (common laborers, musicians, dancers, etc.). Casteism says that if you are born of a Brahmana family, then you are a Brahmana, no matter whether you truly exhibit the genuine characteristics of a Brahmana or not. And if you are born in a Kshatriya family, or a Vaishya or Shudra family, then that is what you must be. It is as if when one is born in a doctor's family, the child is also considered a doctor. However, anyone knows that to become a doctor requires the proper training and perception to see if the child will be a qualified doctor or not. Just being born in the family of a doctor does not mean that the children will also be doctors, although this may help. But they surely are not doctors merely by birth. Training and intelligence must be there. And before training, there also must be the proclivity, tendency, and attraction to even be a doctor. Without that, no amount of training will be of much use because the student will still not want to be, or qualify to be a doctor. Therefore, this form of modern day casteism is useless.

This form of materialistic casteism was practiced five hundred years ago, during the time of Sri Caitanya Mahaprabhu, who was considered an incarnation of the Supreme Being. However, Sri Caitanya paid no mind to these social customs. He saw them as a way that the hereditary Brahmanas were merely protecting their own position and privileges and not spreading spiritual well-being, which is their duty. Even during that time the Brahmanas had the idea that if they ate with or touched anyone outside the Brahmana caste, they would risk losing their own social rank. Sri Caitanya, however, ignored such restrictions and readily accepted invitations to eat with the sincere devotees of the Lord, or also embrace them, even if they were of the lowest social position. To Sri Caitanya, it was their devotion that gave them whatever qualification they needed. In this way, He dismissed the materialistic method of casteism. By this action He also showed that it was not birth that was important, but one's consciousness, intentions, and spiritual awareness that was the prominent factor, which superseded the rank of one's body or family. It is this which actually determines one's personality, character, and abilities, not merely one's birth. This is actually how we should see people and treat them equally as spiritual beings inside material bodies.

WHAT IS THE ORIGINAL VEDIC SYSTEM CALLED VARNASHRAMA

There is much discussion regarding the caste system of India and whether it is an oppressive, dogmatic arrangement meant to keep low class people from moving upwards in society. This needs to be clarified because many people seem to have a great misunderstanding about it. In the cities in India, this influence of the caste system is falling by the wayside, yet it is still found to have some prevalence in the villages and rural areas. I have always said that it is not the culture of India that causes its problems, but it is the forgetfulness, the misinterpretations, misunderstandings, and the distancing from it by society that leaves the gaps wherein flows many errors and misconceptions regarding it. So let us take a deeper look at it.

The original Vedic system called varnashrama was legitimate and virtuous. It is different than the present caste system we find today, which classifies people merely based on their birth, or the caste of their parents. Varnashrama, on the other hand, is the Vedic system that divides society into four natural groups depending on individual characteristics and dispositions. It was meant for the progressive organization of society. Everyone has certain tendencies by their own natural inclinations and choice. These inclinations are also seen in one's occupational preferences, what a person is naturally attracted towards or prefers to do. So there is nothing unusual or forceful about it. These activities are divided into four basic divisions called *varnas*. *Varna* literally means color, relating to the color or disposition of one's consciousness, and, thus, one's likelihood of preferring or showing various tendencies for a particular set of occupations. This would not be determined simply by one's birth, but by one's proclivities, interests and talents as observed by the teachers in the school that the student was attending. This means that it would be determined by one's *guna* and karma. So we need to clear up right now that varna does not refer to skin color, although some people think so, which is a wrong interpretation of the word.

Let us also point out that this kind of counseling was used not only in the Vedic schools of yesterday, but is found in most schools in the west as well. With school tests and counseling to determine the aptitude of the student, the counselors suggest and prepare a type of education or classes to prepare the student for whatever occupation is best for that person, with the idea of preparing him for the college courses he or she would need to graduate fully qualified to pursue a satisfying career. In that way, the person would be most able to be happy and satisfied in their career, and also provide the best contribution to the community and benefit to society. This was the same goal and purpose of the varna system in the Vedic culture.

Guna means the particular mode of material nature which is most predominant in one's character, which is either *sattva-guna*, or the mode of goodness wherein peace and thoughtfulness are observed, or *raja-guna*, when the mode of passion, activity and creativity is apparent, and *tamo-guna*, wherein the mode of ignorance or inertia is seen. One's karma in this case means the inherent tendencies and familiarities with which a person has naturally been born.

For example, there are those who prefer to offer service to society through physical labor or working for others in exchange for payment or certain facilities, or who like to work in forms of self-expression through various ways like dance and music. Such persons are called Shudras. Then there are those who work through agriculture, trade, commerce, business, and banking or administrative work, called Vaishyas. Those who have the talents of leaders, government administration, police or military, and the tendency for the protection of society are called Kshatriyas. And those who are by nature intellectuals, contemplative, teachers, or inspired by acquiring spiritual and philosophical knowledge, and motivated to work in this way for the rest of society are called the Brahmanas. It was never a factor of whether a person had a certain ancestry or birth that determined which class was most appropriate for him or her, although being born in a particular family or tribe would give a natural likelihood to continue in the same line of activity or work. But this was not something that was forced.

The four main *ashramas* divided society for spiritual reasons. These were Brahmacharya (students), Grihasthas (householders), Vanaprasthas (the retired stage, at which time a person begins to give up materialistic pursuits and focus on spiritual goals), and Sannyasa (those who were renounced from all materialistic affairs, usually toward the end of their lives, and completely dedicated to spiritual activities). The first two ashramas, which are the Brahmacarya and Grihastha ashramas, pertain to Pravritti Marga, or the path of action or work. The later two ashramas, Vanaprastha and Sannyasa, pertain to Mivritti Marga, or the path of renunciation or withdrawal from the world. This provided a general pattern for one's life in which people could work out their desires and develop spiritually at the same time.

In this way, the system of varnashrama came into existence according to the natural tendencies of people, and to direct them so that everyone could work together according to the needs of society. The *ashramas* divided an individual's life so that a person could fulfill all of one's basic desires as well as accomplish the spiritual goals of life. Only according to one's qualities, tendencies, and traits, usually as one grew up in school, was it determined which varna was best for that person, after witnessing their actions and interactions with others. And then he would be trained accordingly to do the most suited work that fit his qualities, much like the way counselors work with students in schools today. Thus, he or she would have a suitable occupation which he would enjoy, grow and develop, and make a respectable contribution to society.

In this way, the real purpose of the system of varnashrama was not to label or restrict someone, or classify a person merely based on one's birth or family. It was actually part of the means for self-discovery and development. It was to assist a person to find their place in life where he or she would be most comfortable in terms of functionality and occupation. It was to allow the means for everyone to work according to their own nature, which helps bring happiness to the individual and society. Thus, a person could study what was most suited for him or her rather than pursue a type of work that was not really in line with that person's character or consciousness, and in which he would soon be dissatisfied. So, this would help guide one to more efficiently complete one's life and reach fulfillment. Therefore, the varnashrama system is based on the natural divisions within society and is not meant to establish forced distinctions or restrictions.

However, beyond this it was meant to help raise the consciousness of humanity from materialism to a higher state of devotional regard for God in spiritual life. It would help one in managing the physical, mental, intellectual, and spiritual energy for improving one's health, mental and physical development, and productivity, along with spiritual awareness. Thus, it was meant for assisting society to become spiritually harmonized and make the everyday tasks into a means of spiritual progress and growth.

To explain further, in *Bhagavad-gita* (*Bg.* 4.13) Lord Krishna says, "According to the three modes of material nature (*gunas*) and the work ascribed to them (karma), the four divisions of human society were created by Me." Then He continues, "Brahmanas, Kshatriyas, Vaishyas and Shudras are distinguished by their qualities of work in accordance with the modes of nature (*gunas*)." (*Bg.*18.41) Herein we can see that there is no mention of birth as a determining factor for one's *varna* or classification. They are ascertained by their qualities of work. Furthermore, "By following his qualities of work, every man can become perfect. . . By worship of the Lord, who is the source of all beings and who is all-pervading, man can, in the performance of his own duty [or occupation], attain perfection." (*Bg.*18.45-6)

Herein we can understand that these divisions are created by the Lord so that everyone can be rightly situated in the work and activities that are most suitable for each person, and in which they can feel most comfortable. Whatever occupational tendency a person may have is determined by the modes of material nature one has acquired, or in which he or she associates. Beyond this, these classifications are to organize society in a way that can help in the systematic development of the spiritual consciousness of all mankind.

In the *Vishnu Purana* (3.8.9) Lord Parasharama also says, "The Supreme Lord Vishnu is worshiped by the proper execution of prescribed duties in the system of varna and ashrama. There is no other way to satisfy the Lord." So, by engaging in this varnashrama system the Supreme Lord can be satisfied with one's occupation. It is a way of making one's work and activities into devotional service to the Lord. However, it may be pointed out that a person in pure spiritual consciousness is above all such designations, even though for his service to God he may act in any one of these divisions at any given time. Devotional service to the Lord is never restricted by any classification of actions. Any activity becomes completely spiritual when it is an expression of one's devotion or love of God.

Now we can understand how the Vedic arrangement of varnashrama provides the means for each person in each varna to be able to make spiritual advancement by offering one's activities to the Lord. It is the way a person can directly engage in bhakti-yoga, or devotional service to the Supreme. Thus, in whatever position one is in, all of one's duties can become an offering of love to God, which becomes the highest level of meditation, intention, or activity.

This is confirmed by Suta Gosvami who says in the *Srimad-Bhagavatam* (1.2.8) that such occupational duties a man performs according to his own position are only so much useless labor if they do not provoke attraction for the message of the Supreme Personality of Godhead. This means that the modern materialistic form of casteism that we find today is no longer connected with the Vedic system of varnashrama. It misses the point of helping everyone make spiritual advancement by focusing on our spiritual identity of being the soul within the body, or to please the Supreme Lord. Thus, the caste system as it is today has become simply a materialistic, useless, and destructive system.

An example of this point can be found in the *Bhagavad-gita* (18.42) where Lord Krishna explains that the natural qualities of the Brahmanas are peacefulness, self-control, austerity, purity, tolerance, honesty, wisdom, and knowledge. The *Mahabharata* (Vana Parva, Chapter 180) also goes on with a quote from Yudhisthira, that a Brahmana possesses truthfulness, charity, forgiveness, sobriety, gentleness, austerity, and a lack of hatred. The *Mahabharata* also explains that a Brahmana must be perfectly religious. He must be truthful and able to control his senses. He must execute severe austerities and be detached, humble and tolerant. He must not envy anyone, and must be expert in performing religious sacrifices and giving whatever he has in charity. He must be fixed in devotional service and expert in

Vedic knowledge. These are the twelve qualifications for a Brahmana.

So, unfortunately, in today's form of casteism, when we see Brahmanas who are proud of their position, or who desire material benefit, or look condescendingly at those of lower castes, they are not really elevated but are materialistic. This means that they have lost the true qualities of Brahmanas. They actually help promote contempt through casteism, and take advantage of it for their own purposes. Thus, for those who act this way, and not all of them do, only by birth are they called Brahmanas, but the necessary qualifications are not found in them. In fact, the very people that may pride themselves for their high social classifications, and are supposed to be the spiritual leaders of society (the Brahmanas) only indicate their lack of qualifications by focusing on the temporary material designations when they are supposed to be above such things.

Nonetheless, if everyone engages their talents and tendencies in his or her particular occupation with the idea that it is a service to God, which is the ultimate purpose of the Vedic form of the varnashrama system, then that occupation can also become the means for one's worship and thoughts or meditation on the Supreme. If one thinks like this always, then, by the grace of the Lord, he will be delivered from material existence and attain liberation. This is the highest perfection of life. So, in whatever occupation people may be engaged, if they serve the Supreme Lord in this way, they will achieve this highest level of success. So, it is not that any activity is considered higher or lower, at least in the true Vedic system. It is by this means that the spiritual form of varnashrama can satisfy the Lord and society in general at the same time, and everyone makes spiritual advancement as well. Then ideally, as society progresses in this way, all working together for the satisfaction of the Lord, they forget who is in what position, or that there seems to be a difference, because spiritually they are all transcendental. Thus, everyone rises above the material platform by dint of their spiritual work in devotional service. Then the harmonious and advanced nature of the mode of goodness, as found in the age of Satya-yuga, can be invoked even in this dark age of Kali-yuga.

THE FOUR VARNAS ARE HERE TO STAY

The system of varnashrama exists naturally everywhere because people will always have the tendencies for what they want to do, or have particular qualities for occupational skills. And these can invariably be divided into the four above-mentioned categories. This is natural, and, as we have seen in the evidence here, it has been formed by the Supreme Creator. Therefore, it will always be in existence in some shape or form.

This system, however, was never meant to divide people according to materialistic classifications. It was meant to unite people in a cooperative society in the service of God. In Vedic times, even the Shudras had the same rights as those of the other varnas, and their dignity was preserved without discrimination. In this way, everyone would be satisfied materially and work in a way for the Lord's pleasure. The Vedic culture, ultimately, was for the well-being and spiritual advancement of the whole society. Forced designation or labels like untouchability was never a part of the Vedic process. The materialistic caste system of the present-day has deteriorated into a means of dividing society according to mere parentage or birth, called *jati*, and this kind of discrimination does seem to control certain groups, while protecting or expanding the privileges and happiness of the higher castes. Therefore, this is a misinterpretation of the Vedic customs and a social disease, and was not part of the Vedic system. When it comes to those who are known as "untouchables," actually there is no word as "untouchable" in any of the Vedic scriptures. This is merely a modern and unjust invention.

Logically speaking, if a person is not performing any unhygienic activities, then why should he be called an untouchable simply because of the family in which he was born? Even after performing something dirty, one need only wash oneself properly to be clean again. Likewise, to raise one's consciousness to a higher awareness or frequency of activity, one need only participate in the Vedic methods of spiritual advancement, which must be done regardless of one's rank or varna, whether Shudra or Brahmana.

On the other hand, I have seen Brahmanas in India who ate eggs, meat, and drank alcohol, all of which are considered to be dirty or contaminating habits. How does one clean oneself from that if he is considered a clean and pure Brahmana? It means that such a person is hardly a Brahmana at all, even if he is born in a Brahmana family. So classification is to be judged by qualities, habits, and the content of one's character, not by mere title and birth.

So, as it stands today, the present form of casteism is a great curse on Hinduism and Vedic culture. It attacks the core of its spiritual philosophy, and has resulted in large numbers of Hindus converting to other religions in an attempt to become free of it. Therefore, it needs to be changed or simply thrown out completely and replaced by the genuine system of occupational categories, or varnashrama. However, there are already spiritual institutions or groups of Vedic followers who have set the proper example and are open to everyone, and do not divide people or consider them according to their birth or social status. The members of such organizations all view each other as equals working together for spiritual cooperation and advancement, all using their talents in whatever way suits them best for the purpose of upliftment for everyone.

THE EARLIEST REFERENCE TO THE VARNAS

The earliest reference to the varnas is found in the Purusha Sukta verses of the *Rig-veda* (Book Ten, Hymn 90). There are those who refer to these verses as justification for the modern caste system. But let us take a closer look at them.

In these verses, it is described that the great sages worship the Purusha, or the Supreme Soul, Lord of immortality, and from whom the universe is created. In worshiping the Purusha, whose form is completely spiritual and transcendental, the sages can see how all other aspects of the creation are also manifest. Within Him are all other deities and demigods and rishis. From this ritual, all other *Richas* and *Sama* hymns are born from the Purusha, and from Him come all other creatures, and animals, and so on. Then this hymn explains that from the Purusha's mouth, arms, thighs, and feet come the human beings. The Brahmana was His mouth, the Rajas or Kshatriyas were both of His arms, His thighs became the Vaishyas, and from His feet the Shudras were produced.

After that it is described how the Moon was gendered from his mind [connecting its affects with mental activities], and the sun came from His eye [providing vision]. Indra and Agni also came from His mouth and Vayu [the wind god] came from His breath. From His navel came mid-air, sky from His head, earth from His feet, and regions from His ear.

Thus, we find that a variety of items are identified with parts of His body. However, this does not mean that there is a classificational difference between what is lower and what is higher. It mostly distinguishes the different functions of each entity in its association with the various parts of the Purusha. The Purusha's or Lord's body is completely spiritual. For those who understand this point, it means that there is no difference between His head, hand, thighs, feet, mind, breath, eye, ear, and so on. Let us emphasize that they are all made of the same spiritual qualities, and one aspect or limb can perform the same function as any other aspect. They are all pure consciousness. Thus, it does not mean that the Brahmanas are necessarily a higher classification than the Vaishyas or Shudras, but that they naturally have different functions.

The point is that every living being is considered a part of the Lord's body. As verse three of the Purusha Sukta explains, all creatures are one-fourth of Him. In other words, they all have a place in the Lord's form, they all belong, and they all have a duty to perform, and should be respected as such. It means that they all have a purpose, and that all parts of the body must work together. In the same way, the social body of society must all work together in order for it to function properly and harmoniously. Being parts of the spiritual body of the Purusha, all living beings are also ultimately completely spiritual in essence. That essence is what we must understand, for that essence is of the same essential spiritual quality as the Lord. That is what connects us all together and with God.

Another aspect of this is that in the Second verse of the Purusha Sukta Prayers, it explains that the Purusha expands with food. This food is indicative of the worship, the sacrificial offerings or meditative devotions of mankind. Thus, for society to reach its zenith of spiritual potential, they must all cooperate in working together in devotion to God. This means that society, being different parts of the body of God, must all act while having God as the center, just as our own body must work to serve the central part of it, which is the stomach. If the feet, legs, arms, and head do not cooperate to feed the stomach, then the whole body, including all its parts, becomes weak and dysfunctional, and then dies. It does not matter which part may be considered the most important, if they do not all work to make sure the stomach is fed, then they all get weak and die. In the same way, the different parts of the body of society must all work together or it becomes weak and its practical purpose and functionality begin to die out.

So, as explained in this prayer, the body of the Purusha expands and grows strong when all of its parts, namely mankind, work for the common cause, which is to cooperate together, seeing each person as part of the body of God, and act in devotion to the Lord. That is the ultimate goal, as emphasized in the Vedic tradition. In other words, you cannot please God if, by perceiving our differences, we do not act harmoniously together with God as the center. These are but a few of the lessons we can get from the Purusha Sukta Prayers in the *Rig-veda*. Now we must act on them and recognize each other in the proper perspective as spiritual beings, and working for the benefit of the whole and for God. That is the real purpose of the Vedic varnashrama system.

HOW THE PRESENT CASTEISM DEVELOPED

In the Vedic times it was perfectly all right for a person to change their classification or varna by switching their profession. It provided that kind of flexibility. Thus, on occasion, the upper class Brahmanas might become warriors or kings, while the lower class Shudras could also become scholars or saints, depending on their ability, qualifications, and the circumstance. However, only later did the divisions of the four varnas become less flexible, thus causing one's birth to be one's class.

Over time the fourfold varna system became divided into many hundreds and thousands of other varnas, castes or jatis. Most of such jatis are people of a particular geographical or linguistic region. Thus, each member within a varna would often act accordingly and marry amongst others within that varna. However, Kshatriyas were often excluded from such nuances.

So how did the form of casteism that we find today develop? Traditionally, it is related in the

Srimad-Bhagavatam (1.18.32-50): "Once upon a time [about 5000 years ago] Maharaja Pariksit, while engaged in hunting in the forest with bow and arrows, became extremely fatigued, hungry and thirsty while following the stags. While searching for a reservoir of water, he entered the hermitage of the well-known Shamika Rishi and saw the sage sitting silently with eyes closed. The muni's sense organs, breath, mind, and intelligence were all restrained from material activities, and he was situated in a trance apart from the three [wakefulness, dream and unconsciousness], having achieved a transcendental position qualitatively equal with the Supreme Absolute.

"The sage, in meditation, was covered by the skin of a stag, and long, compressed hair was scattered all over him. The King, whose palate was dry from thirst, asked him for water. The King, not received by any formal welcome by means of being offered a seat, place, water and sweet addresses, considered himself neglected, and so thinking in this way, he became angry. The King's anger and envy, directed toward the Brahmana sage, were unprecedented, being that circumstances had made him hungry and thirsty.

"While leaving, the King, being so insulted, picked up a lifeless snake with his bow and angrily placed it on the shoulder of the sage [as an insult]. Then he returned to his palace. Upon returning, he began to contemplate and argue within himself whether the sage had actually been in meditation, with senses concentrated and eyes closed, or whether he had just been feigning trance just to avoid receiving a lower Kshatriya [meaning someone lower in varna or caste].

"The sage had a son, Shringi, who was very powerful, being a Brahmana's son. While he was playing with inexperienced boys, he heard of his father's distress, which was caused by the King. Then and there the boy spoke as follows: 'O just look at the sins of the rulers who, like crows and watchdogs at the door, perpetrate sins against their masters, contrary to the principles governing servants. The descendants of the kingly orders are definitely designated as watchdogs, and they must keep themselves at the door. On what grounds can dogs enter the house and claim to dine with the master on the same plate? After the departure of Sri Krishna, the Personality of Godhead and supreme ruler of everyone, these upstarts have flourished, our protector being gone. Therefore, I myself shall take up this matter and punish them. Just witness my power.'

"The son of the rishi, his eyes red-hot with anger, touched the water of the river Kaushika while speaking to his playmates and discharged the following thunderbolt of words and cursed the King: 'On the seventh day from today a snake-bird will bite the most wretched one of that dynasty [Maharaja Pariksit] because of his having broken the laws of etiquette by insulting my father.'

"Thereafter, when the boy returned to the hermitage, he saw a snake on his father's shoulder, and out of his grief he cried very loudly. The rishi, born in the family of Angira Muni, gradually opened his eyes hearing his son crying, and saw the dead snake around his neck. He threw the dead snake away [thinking nothing of it] and asked his son why he was crying, whether anyone had done him any harm. On hearing this, the son explained to him what had happened.

"The father heard from his son that the King had been cursed, although he should never have been condemned, for he was the best amongst all human beings. The rishi did not congratulate his son, but, on the contrary, began to repent, saying: 'Alas! What a great sinful act was performed by my son. He has awarded heavy punishment for an insignificant offense. O my boy, your intelligence is immature, and therefore you have no knowledge that the king, who is the best amongst human beings, is as good as the Personality of Godhead. He is never to be placed on an equal footing with common men. The citizens of the state live in prosperity, being protected by his unsurpassable prowess.

"My dear boy, the Lord, who carries the wheel of a chariot, is represented by the monarchical regime, and when this regime is abolished the whole world becomes filled with thieves, who then at once vanquish the unprotected subjects like scattered lambs. Due to the termination of the monarchical regimes, and the plundering of the people's wealth by rogues and thieves, there will be great social disruptions. People will be killed and injured, and animals and women will be stolen. And for all these sins, we [the Brahmana class] shall be responsible.

"At that time the people in general will fall systematically from the path of a progressive civilization [the Vedic culture] in respect to the qualitative engagements of the castes and the orders of society and the Vedic instructions. Thus, they will be more attracted to economic development for sense gratification, and as a result there will be an unwanted population on the level of dogs and monkeys."

This was an arrangement by the Lord, or providence if you will, so that Maharaja Pariksit would depart from home and prepare to leave his body. However, Shringi, the powerful yet immature Brahmana boy, came under the lower influences of Kali-yuga, such as pride and envy, which a Brahmana is never meant to feel. It was through this incident that the degrading age of Kali-yuga was waiting for to spoil the Vedic cultural heritage of the four orders or varnas of life. It was this incident which was the first time, through an unqualified Brahmana boy, that the higher castes felt dislike or hatred for the lower castes. Thus, the first victim of Brahminical injustice was Maharaja Pariksit.

By the influence of Kali-yuga, the son of a Brahmana, under the influence of his young playmates, became proud of the power he had and wrongly compared a qualified king to crows and watchdogs. Thus, the downfall of the Brahminical powers started as the Brahmanas began to give more importance to birthright than to culture. In this way, the protection that was provided by the King against the onslaught of Kali-yuga became slackened, and, thereafter, all of the other castes or varnas, all the people in general, began to neglect their duties and lose qualifications. Thus, the Vedic culture started to decline. And because of this, people of the lower varnas also gradually became envious of the higher varnas, and then disunity, disrespect, and friction slowly increased through the years amongst the castes.

The boy's father realized all this and explained that now, because of the stupid and sinful act of his son, all of society would begin to move in a behavior contrary to the spiritually progressive way of life.

In this way, through time, society began to deviate from the Vedic standards. The perverted nature of the modern caste system started to creep into the genuine Vedic system of varnashrama, even from the time of Jamadagni and Parashurama many hundreds of years ago. As the Brahmanas became more self-interested, a struggle began between them and the Kshatriyas. The Brahmanas made birth in a Brahmana's family as the qualification for being one. Thus, one's varna was determined by birth, which stifled people in the lower varnas. The varna system, which was absent from the Vedic literature, was included and explained only in the Dharmasastras and smriti literature, such as the *Manu-samhita*.

In this way, the varnashrama system degenerated in India, and all the classes gradually began to neglect their duties. Testing the abilities, tendencies, and talents of the children to determine their natural interests and character disappeared. Birth became the major factor in determining varna or caste. The Brahmanas in particular became self-centered and protective of their superiority, forgetting their duties and losing their qualities. Sacrifice, religious study, and austerity gradually faded in the traits of many of the Brahmanas. The people in the other varnas also lost their good characteristics. Chivalry, leadership, and forbearance were no longer to be found to such a high degree in the

Kshatriya spirit. As leaders, they no longer kept the welfare of the people in focus. Vaishyas lost their charity and honesty in business and became greedy and avaricious. The laborer class, the Shudras, no longer wanted to be servants, but desired that others serve them. They wanted to have position and control, without knowing what is best to do with it, and not being qualified to guide or lead people properly, and, thus, misdirecting the world. In this way, society has become disheveled and out of balance and harmony, and does not follow in accord with Vedic Dharma.

Some of the Kshatriyas rebelled and formed or joined Buddhism, which did without all varnas or castes. The Vaishyas also used Jainism. Together, Buddhism and Jainism tried to bring the end of Brahmanism. The result was actually a deterioration of the Vedic culture in general.

As society in India started to decay after distancing itself from the true Vedic system, and because of disunity and friction, it weakened to the point wherein it allowed the low-born or mleccha kings [those who observed no form of Vedic standards, or even disrespected it] from outside India to come in and conquer and control it. This brought even further decline to the Vedic culture. Later, it was during the British reign in which the modern caste system became more widely practiced and ingrained in Hinduism. By now the caste system was completely different and separate from the Vedic system of varnashrama. The British encouraged the practice of casteism to increase the divisions between people, thus making it easier for the British to rule over them. A disunited society will hardly have the force, cooperation, or strength to defend itself from intruders. So the British fueled casteism and kept it more ingrained in society for their own interests. In this way, it was many years before the British could be removed. In fact, the British justified their presence with promises of helping keep the peace between the growing divisions in the Indian social structure. In any case, well after the British left, the divisions and the focus on ethnic classifications that had increased during their reign have remained.

So, the British used the untouchable classes as a means for their own political purpose, and an instrument in their divide and rule policy for dividing the Hindu majority. This amplified the divisions of the caste system and made them more solid in the people's identification with the castes. This had negative and regressive affects on the Indian society that have not gone away. However, in 1936, the Indian government made it even worse by outlining the Scheduled Castes among the untouchables and labeled a list of such classifications. The various castes would be regarded with separate status for assembly and seats of parliament, along with special benefits for education and employment. This became adopted into the Indian Constitution which has made it a practice that has endured to date, with special laws making the labeling of untouchability an offense. The Untouchability Act of 1955 provides the list of penalties for any such offense. Now, there are numerous and separate divisions amongst the Scheduled Castes to the point where it will never cease to exist, at least in a general way, especially in the villages. The cities are becoming somewhat more homogenized due to necessity of occupational fulfillment and education as opposed to merely growing out of such traditions.

As far as "untouchablitiy" goes, it was never mentioned in any Vedic literature. This was never a part of the Vedic system, but merely a more modern invention. There is no justification for it. The earliest mention of it seems to be in the Chinese traveler Fa Hsien's account of his journey in the 4th century CE. It also seems that this became a name for those who were not amongst the basic four varnas, and were thus without a caste or varna. They were called Panchama in some regions, which merely means the fifth varna. Later, in 1933, Gandhi gave them the name of Harijan, or "people of God", which was accepted by many members of the

Panchama class. The 1931 census used the term of "Scheduled Castes" as the proper name for identifying the Panchama class. In 1970, the term "Dalit" came to be used, which is a Marathi word based in Sanskrit which means "broken or ground down," usually meaning one who is oppressed. This term has slowly gained usage across India.

Though Indian society has always been progressive to varying degrees, this idea of assigning a varna, caste or class of activity to someone merely by one's birth parents has been the major failure of individual and social development in modern Hindu society.

THE DANGERS OF CASTEISM AS WE FIND IT TODAY

As casteism continues, it furthers the fragmentation of Indian society. In fact, you could say that it has practically killed Vedic society and has brought about the numerous divisions and social quarrels that we now find in India. Even amongst the Hindus alone, there has been fighting along caste, ethnic, and sectarian lines for hundreds of years. This is one of the main reasons why the country has been weakened to such a degree that they could not properly defend themselves in a unified way from the genocide under the Muslim invasions, and now modern fundamentalism. This sort of fragmentation also forced Indians to endure two centuries of British persecutions.

Casteism today does not help society advance spiritually. In fact, it helps promote emphasis on bodily and social distinctions, contempt, and disapproval among the people of different classes and ethnic groups. For this reason, we still see today that when the Shudras and Dalits feel like they are disliked by fellow Hindus, they become Muslims, Christians, or Buddhists in the attempt to find greater acceptance and avoid class differences. The result of this has been social disharmony. Otherwise, there would have been no need for parts of India to be divided to create Bangladesh and Pakistan, which have since become nothing more than mortal enemies of India. Have any lessons been learned? Apparently not. Ethnic intolerance is on the rise in various parts of India.

Even today you can find such divisions that a Brahmana from one state does not trust a Brahmana from a different part of India. For example, the Nambudris of Kerala look down on any other Brahmanas. Even among other groups, a Jat boy from the Punjab will not marry a Jat girl from Uttar Pradesh. And a Patel from Kutch will look at a Patel from Ahmedabad as foreign. Thus, the problem of caste and ethnicity is making a society that fights like cats and dogs. In reality, casteism is killing Indian culture.

WHAT WE CAN DO TO ELIMINATE THE MODERN CASTE SYSTEM

Social revolutionaries who wanted to change the modern caste system have been around for a long time. Gandhi was a notable figure in this. However, before him was Ramanujacharya. He crusaded against the concept of untouchability. In Melkote, Karanataka, he threw open the doors to the temple and let everyone in, regardless of classification. Sri Caitanya Mahaprabhu also ignored the restrictions that were established by the caste system. He associated and ate with anyone who was a sincere devotee of the Lord, considering one's intention and consciousness as being more important than the mere social classification of one's body.

So what can be done to change this form of casteism? We can go back to the Vedic system of studying the natural tendencies of the child in its early stage of education. Then observe the child's association, activities and intellectual interests to begin to determine his or her real varna or direction in occupation. Then, as in any western country, as the child grows, begin testing, counseling and steering it in the proper course of education to determine if the right category has been given. Then allow that person to develop him or herself to the fullest possibility without restrictions of some forced caste placed on the person. It does not even have to be called varnashrama. But the process can merely direct a person according to his or her qualities and characteristics to find more fulfillment and potential in life, and, thus, more happiness. This is only the basics of what varnashrama was and is meant to do.

Other things that can be done that can help do away with the modern form of casteism include the following:

1. ENFORCING THE EXISTING LAWS. There have been laws passed against the practice of untouchability and discrimination toward those considered to be of lower caste, some of which have already been enacted. India's Constitution has a specific Article forbidding untouchability (Article 17), along with Article 25(2b) to throw open Hindu religious institutions to all sections of Hindus, and Article 15 (4) to permit the state to make special provisions for Scheduled Castes, Scheduled Tribes and Other Backward Classes. However, this has only made the caste system more ingrained in society, making it more difficult to fix or do away with. It also has a host of other Articles in Part III to ensure Right to Equality. After all, India is a democracy with freedom for anyone regardless of race, religion or sex. And under a democracy, everyone should follow the same set of laws--a uniform code for all Indians. However, these laws need to be monitored in a way to make sure that they are implemented to see to it that this caste prejudice is not only outlawed, but stopped. After all, India still receives much criticism for this from the global community.

Is this possible? Yes, it is. Nepal, on August 16, 2001, recently made the announcement that they would put such laws into practice against the discrimination of lower-caste Hindus and the centuries-old idea that certain people are untouchable, which would become punishable by a severe sentence.

2. FREEDOM TO ENTER ALL HINDU TEMPLES. All people, no matter whether they are so-called Dalits, other low-caste Hindus, or people like Westerners who have converted to Sanatana-dharma, should have the means and freedom which enable them to enter all Vedic temples and participate in the Vedic process of spiritual development. This practice of restricting who can enter temples is merely a practice that expands and protects the rights of those who are already privileged, without showing the concern for others. It is another example of how the upper-castes suppress those of lower status. It is another example of how it is causing the disintegration of the noble standards that were once found in the traditional Vedic culture.

The point is that if everyone can equally participate in the worship and traditions that you find in the Vedic temples, which is indeed possible in most temples in India, it helps preserve, protect, and promote Sanatana-dharma and the Vedic traditions. And everyone has a right to follow and participate. This is what must be upheld. Then people will not feel inclined to convert to another religion, and will remain within their own customs. Otherwise, if such things as restrictions to enter temples continue, it only helps provide a prescription for a slow extinction of the Vedic culture.

3. STOP ALL BONDED LABOR. Furthermore, the practice of bonded labor should be not only outlawed, but with stiff fines and penalties for those who still utilize it. Bonded labor is the practice of using poor villagers for cheap labor, often giving them low wages and shambles for dwellings. Then giving them loans with interest that are supposed to be paid off in exchange for labor. If the loans are not paid off, then the person's children must also work for years in order to try to pay off the loans of their fathers or grandfathers. This can go on for generations. It is essentially financial slavery. You see bonded labor in places like textile shops, large farms, and in the carpet and silk factories, which are known to be the prominent places that use child labor. It is not only time for the government to get involved to make sure that this practice comes to an end once and for all, and see to it that all financial obligations are nullified, but make sure that all who continue this practice are penalized severely enough. It is another example of how the rich and privileged suppress and control the lower classes.

In the real system of varnashrama, everyone's position can be respected since everyone is seen as servants of the Lord in whatever capacity they serve. The people are appreciated for what they do. Workers and laborers were never to be treated harshly, or given hellish conditions in which to live or work. They were to be treated kindly and fairly.

4. PROTECT ALL VILLAGE CHILDREN. Another thing that must be stopped in this connection is the practice of bribing or purchasing tribal or poor village girls with the promise of good jobs and then taking them to places like Mumbai where they are sold and forced into prostitution. Many of the girls in the sex trade in Mumbai are not there by choice, but because they were kidnapped and then beaten, starved, or tortured into submission. This goes on not only for the profit, but because of the corruption in the local governments and police departments that allow it to continue. There is no reason why the government and police cannot stop this if they really wanted. There are laws against this but no one implements them. They could easily close the houses of prostitution overnight and free these girls, except for the bribes and the corruption that allows the Indian mafia to take advantage of these young girls.

This ruins the lives of many young girls and their families, helps spread diseases like HIV-AIDS through India, and is another point for which India receives much criticism, while the international community watches. Therefore, heavy punishment should be administered to anyone for such kidnapping or bribery, and the madams who run the houses of prostitution should be sent to long terms of prison. All politicians or police commissioners who do not carry out the laws to stop this, or who accept bribes to look the other way, should also be relieved of their position or jailed for long periods of time. This would have immediate effects.

5. STOP THE DOWRY SYSTEM. The concept of dowry should also be abolished, not merely by the laws that have been established, but by enforcement with stiff fines when it is found to have taken place. Dowry was originally a way of helping the newly married couple get off to a good start financially, and for the groom to help protect the bride if something should happen to him. Now it has become a perverted system in which it is the bride's parents who must fork over a large dowry to the agreement of the groom and his family. If the dowry is not large enough, there is either no marriage, or the bride is treated terribly later on. This system helps divide the classes and puts the financial burden on the bride's family to have their daughter get married. It is especially difficult when the bride's family is poor, or has a number of daughters that need to get married. It also turns the marriage into a business arrangement between families rather than a sacred institution between husband and wife. It is also a big factor in the abuse of women and bride burnings in India. This system is another reason for the increased rate of infanticide and abortions when it is discovered that a woman is pregnant with a girl. The present-day system of dowry is now mostly a materialistic and shameful arrangement.

6. PROMOTE GENUINE SPIRITUAL KNOWLEDGE. Ultimately, as with all social problems, the most important action to take in order to change society is to provide the means for continued spiritual development. That is why it is important that spiritual organizations work to fulfill the above-mentioned points, and also provide the means for the upliftment of people's consciousness through spiritual education and practice, so that people can seriously change their view of their fellow human beings. That is why temples need to be open to everyone. We all need to realize our transcendental identities, and that we are all spiritual beings, not the temporary bodies in which we reside. As spiritual beings, we are all the same. On that level, there needs to be no special treatment of one over another. Materially, there may be so many differences, but these are all temporary and only within the material vision. By recognizing this, it can help us get back to practicing the real and genuine version of casteism, which is the Vedic system of varnashrama.

My own spiritual master, Srila A. C. Bhaktivedanta Swami, put it bluntly, he said that if all you see is who is a Brahmana, Kshatriya, Vaishya, or Shudra, then your vision is no better than that of a dog. A dog also recognizes distinctions, such who is its friend, enemy, or source of food. Our vision should be much higher than that if we are to consider ourselves human beings.

At present, we are entering a phase of Indian culture in which, especially in the cities, caste is playing a decreasingly significant role. It is more likely now that people get the jobs they want, careers they are qualified for after appropriate training, living where they want, and so on. This is also the case as Indians move to foreign countries where the younger generations have less regard or even less awareness for the meaning and implication of caste. As we have mentioned, the idea of caste by birth should be abandoned, which we can see is slowly fading. However, varnashrama is part of a legitimate Vedic system that still exists in a natural way, since everyone has basic tendencies and interests, as we have shown, that are part of everyone. And the basic divisions of these interests are described as varnas. It is according to the natural tendencies that make for a person's varna as opposed to their jati or birth situation. This was the way the Vedic system was supposed to be, as we will continue to describe in the following pages.

* * *

The above mentioned points, which are not many, may not completely cure this problem of caste suppression and bonded and child labor, but it could certainly take things in the right direction and begin to change how things in the social arrangement of India continue.

Many organizations have shown and teach disregard for the caste system and its materialistic designations. Spiritual organizations such as Iskcon, the Swami Narayana organization, the Swadhyaya group, the RSS, VHP, and others, have taken the path of showing the equality amongst all people without caste distinctions. They treat everyone equally while allowing individuals to pursue their own particular occupational tendencies without the stigma of being categorized into any certain social group. This is one way in which society can again be unified, especially in regard to Hindu society and India in general.

It is also of utmost importance to use every occasion to help change the social disparities into a common devotional unity. We can especially see such unity at spiritual festivals, like the Kumbha Mela of January, 2001 in Allahabad, or any Kumbha Mela. At this spiritual event, wherein 71 million people attended over a seven week period, everyone bathed in the rivers side by side, both rich and poor, educated and not, villagers and city dwellers alike. They all honored the sages and saints together, or sat in rows together doing puja or listening to the talks, or taking food given at the camps. Social sectarianism had no place in it. So Hindu unity is possible. Yet, we have to be ready to tear down the needless ethnic barriers and unnecessary classifications that get in the way.

We need to have more social gatherings that allow people to come together in a cooperative mood, then work or play together, and get to know each other better. We especially need to have more religious and spiritual functions, like Krishna Janmastami, Ramnavami, etc., that can bring everyone together to celebrate in a way in which we forget about our class distinctions or ethnic divisions. That way we can all be inspired and then leave the event while still holding that inspiration in our hearts. By experiencing such events and then carrying this attitude wherever we go, it will reinforce social harmony, equality and fraternity amongst all.

When you are spiritually charged, you want to share that inspiration and love with everyone. You don't want anything to stifle your feeling of spiritual exhilaration. You want everyone else to feel it, too. That's when you are really approaching true spiritual and God consciousness. And casteism can never be a part of that. It will only separate you from your fellow spiritual beings, and take down your spiritual consciousness and alienate you from God and from the God within everyone.

Another thing that can help in this matter is that swamis from various maths and temples should visit those who are neglected. They should put on religious functions in their communities. Or they can make sure that such people, along with everyone else, are invited to the temples for regular functions, and see to it that there is equality in matters of puja, worship, prasad and food distribution, and Vedic education and instructions. This is the common heritage of all Hindus, and, indeed, all of mankind. No one should be deprived from that, and it should be our duty to see to it that everyone has this opportunity. We must all do our part. Otherwise, if there are any who are not spiritually educated, then we are the ones to blame.

Ironing out these man-made difficulties by spreading spiritual education is, in effect, a way of invoking and showing our devotion to God. If God established varnashrama, as explained in the *Bhagavad-gita*, then we should work in ways to tear down the modern and materialistic caste system and reinstall the genuine Vedic process of the four main orders of society and the justifiable way to determine who is fit for which order. In this Vedic system, everyone is recognized as being spiritually equal, and everyone can work according to their occupational tendencies toward pleasing God without being subject to rigid social classification and stigma.

It is my personal vision of a casteless society, a society that focuses on unity through our spiritual identities, which are all equal and beyond bodily designations. It is my personal vision wherein everyone can work according to their own natural tendencies in a spirit of devotion to God without being categorized merely because of their birth. Like so many others, it is my vision of a society in which everyone can get along, cooperating and assisting each other in harmony toward our spiritual growth. However, we all have to work toward social reform. After all, what kind of world do you want to live in? What kind of world do you prefer? A world divided, full of social disparities and ethnic divisions? Or a world united in cooperation and harmony, all working to encourage and help each other through life? The decision is obvious.

We should all be ambassadors to spread social harmony. We should all be ambassadors of the genuine Vedic standards and culture. We should all be revolutionaries to break the materialistic social barriers between us. We must be willing to work for the progress and upliftment of all, which then guarantees our own upliftment. We must be willing to change society, and that change starts within each and every one of us, and the way we view one another.

CHAPTER TWO

Vedic Literature Says Caste by Birth is Unjust

When it comes to the sensitive topic of varnashrama, or what many people call the caste system of India, we have seen so many talks over this issue, both pro and con, back and forth, this way and that. We all know that the Vedic system of varnashrama has been mentioned in the Vedic literature in many places, such as in the Purusha Sukta verses of the *Rig-veda* (Book Ten, Hymn 90). But there is no indication in these verses that say that birth is the essential quality for one's varna. Yet, it seems that many people still do not understand how the varna system was meant to be implemented, as can be seen in the modern form of the caste system of today. The problem is not because of varnashrama, but because of this misunderstanding of what it really is that has caused so many of India's social problems. This article contains many quotes from Vedic *shastra* to clarify what the varnashrama or caste system is actually supposed to be, which is quite different than what we find today.

As we explained in the previous chapter, there are four basic social divisions, namely the Brahmanas (those who are priests, or interested in the study, teaching and practice of spiritual knowledge and intellectual pursuits), Kshatriyas (those who are soldiers, in the military, or police, politicians, managers, etc.), Vaishyas (merchants, businessmen, bankers, farmers, tradesmen, etc.), and Shudras (those who would rather engage in simple labor or employment, or technicians and other craftsmen in the service of others, etc.). Outcastes are those who are outside these four. There are also the four ashramas of life, which include Brahmacharis (youth, student life, generally celibates), Grihastas (householders), Vanaprasthas (those who are retired from family life), and Sannyasa (the renounced monks, some of whom travel the world to teach). This is the Vedic system of varnashrama.

The modern caste system is seen to usually dictate one's varna or caste merely by one's birth family, as if one automatically inherits the caste of one's father, which is why there is a growing dislike for it. This is not the traditional Vedic system of varnashrama. This is the difference and the problem. The traditional Vedic system calculated one's occupational class by recognizing one's natural talents, interests, tendencies, and abilities. It was similar to the modern system of having high school counselors adjust a student's academic courses by discussing with the students their interests in conjunction with the results of their IQ tests. Thus, such counselors see what occupational direction is best suited for the students so they can achieve a fitting career that is of interest to them, and helps them be a contributor to society at the same time. The councilors would then adjust the student's academic curriculum or course of study in a way that would best fit the occupation the student was striving to attain. The four basic divisions of society, as outlined in the Vedic system, are natural classifications and found everywhere, in every society, call it what you want. Plus, the traditional Vedic varnashrama system was never so inflexible that one could not change from one occupation or class to another. The rigidity of the present-day caste system, based on *jati* or one's birth family, is actually leading us away from the flexibility, and the common sense, of the Vedic varna system.

Another problem with the present day caste system is that an increasing number of adults in India, what to speak of Western countries, who get married to partners who come from different varnas, different family lineages, and various ethnic backgrounds, and become parents. How is it possible then to determine the caste or varna of the child they produce based only on its birth or parentage? So when this increases to additional mixed varnas and *jatis*, caste by birth no longer holds true, if it ever could. It increasingly depends on *guna* and karma, which molds the tendencies, talents, abilities, intelligence level, attractions, and characteristics of the individual. And this cannot be determined until the child engages in actions and interactions among others. Only then is there some indication for what is a person's varna or most likely career classification.

For this reason, you could say that the modern caste system that we find today is actually opposed to the Vedic system of varna. The Vedic process was a matter of bringing experience and wisdom of the ages to assist and direct a person's life in what would be the most productive and satisfying occupation that would fit the mentality, interests, talents, and level of consciousness of an individual. It was never meant to dominate, stifle, hold down, or demean anyone. Therefore, the modern caste system as we find it today should be thrown out, and the natural system of the Vedic varnashrama should be properly understood as it was meant to be.

So, to show what I am talking about, here in the *shastric* quotes that follow I try to provide a clear description of how the varna system was never meant to be based merely on one's family birth, but by one's talents, natural interests, proclivities, expertise, and activities. These quotes are from the Bhrama Parva section of the *Bhavishya Purana* (abbreviated as BP). And no matter how much or how little credit you give to this *Purana*, you still cannot deny the logic with which this information is presented. The verses cited herein from the Bhrama Parva section of the *Bhavishya Purana* are known to be relatively free of corruptions, and its antiquity is vouchsafed as well. The same verses are also repeated verbatim in the *Skanda Purana* (north Indian versions) and a few verses of similar purport are also found in the beginning of the *Shukranatisara*. Some scholars say that the last is a 19th century forgery, but no less than Swami Dayanand Sarasvati acknowledged it as an ancient text, and most scholars date it between 300-1200 CE. So at a minimum, these verses do represent an alternative opinion and an elaboration on the Vedic *varna-jati* system.

In this portion of the *Bhavishya Purana* that follows, the answers to the questions are spoken by Sumantu, the disciple of Srila Vyasadeva, to King Shatanika. This was at the suggestion of Srila Vyasadeva [VedaVyasa] who was sitting nearby in the assembly of sages, all of whom were listening to the discussion. (*Bhavishya Purana*, Bhrama Parva, Chapter 1.28-35)

HOW DO WE RECOGNIZE ONE'S VARNA?

First of all, how do we recognize one's varna is an ancient question, even asked by the sages of the distant past to Lord Brahma. What is it that really makes the difference between one person and the next? "The sages asked: O Lord Brahma, in the beginning of creation, how was one recognized as a Brahmana? Was it because of his birth in a particular family, his knowledge of the *Vedas*, the characteristics of his body, his accomplishment of self-realization, his quality of behavior, or the prescribed duties he carried out? Is it the mind, speech, activities, body, or the qualities that determine one's social status? Surely one's birth in a certain caste [or family] is not sufficient for one to be recognized as a Brahmana. One's qualities and work must also play an important part in determining a person's position in society. The Vedic literature supports this view." (BP, 38.8-11)

"Different social orders, such as the Brahmanas and Kshatriyas (and others) are directly seen, but simply being born in a particular family does not automatically grant one his social status. An intelligent person can easily recognize a horse in the midst of many cows. Similarly, among many who are born in a particular social status, those who are actually qualified in terms of character and activities can be easily recognized. (BP, 38.19-20)

"Some people say that all of humanity is the topmost caste, and there is nothing more to be said than this. They fail to understand that the various purificatory processes, such as the sacred thread ceremony [initiation into the twice-born status], make a person distinct from those who do not undergo such rituals." (BP, 38.21)

Such customs certainly help one progress and is recommended, but the fact remains that in spite of such purificatory rites, we are all still very much the same, as described next.

WE ARE ALL QUITE ALIKE

"How can all the living entities who take birth, grow old, become diseased, and then die, who suffer the threefold miseries of material existence, who take birth in innumerable species, such as human beings, birds, dogs, pigs, dog-eaters, insects, and tortoises, who are all placed into very awkward conditions of life, fraught with danger, illness, lamentation, and distress, and who are constantly being drowned by the burden of their grave sinful reactions, be accepted as qualified Brahmanas?" (BP, 38.23-25)

Therefore, there must be some additional means that can help identify one's mental makeup and high or low level of intellect and consciousness.

IT IS ONLY OUR ACTIONS AND QUALIFICATIONS THAT DIFFERENTIATE US

"Just as one can differentiate between a soldier, an elephant, a horse, a cow, a goat, a camel, and an ass by seeing their colors and forms [as distinguished because of their birth], all living entities have different characteristics and duties that distinguish them from one another." (BP, 38.30)

"[However] the question, 'Who is a Brahmana?' cannot be answered so easily. Actually, there is no question of a person being qualified as a Brahmana simply because he was born in a family of Brahmanas. When a person is designated as belonging to one of the four divisions of the social order [whether it be Kshatriyas, Vaishyas, Shudras or Brahmanas]—that [designation] is not eternal. There is no physical characteristic that enables one to determine who is a Brahmana. A fair or dark complexion, which, after all, is temporary, is no real indication of a person's varna." (BP, 38.31)

In Goswami Tulsidas's *Shri Ramcharitmanas* there are many instances when this issue is also addressed. In the "Sabri episode", Lord Rama speaks to Sabri about the importance of action (Chapter III, Aranya Kand, Verse 34, Line 4,5,6). It is clearly stated that "Bhakti (devotion and unification with the supreme), does not consider caste, religion, etc., rather it is determined by the character and qualities of an individual."

A CASTE SYSTEM BASED ON BIRTH IS UNJUST

"Therefore, the conception of a caste system based solely on birth is artificial and temporary. It may seem to be reality, but that is only due to the influence of the practice of a particular period. A businessman and doctor are both human beings, but their profession is different. Their work is according to their nature and qualities, and not because of the family they were born into." (BP, 38.32)

"Can a person, thus, claim to be a Brahmana if he does not act according to the codes of good conduct? Can a man claim to be a Kshatriya if he does not protect the citizens? Can a person claim to be a Vaishya if he gives up performing his prescribed duties [in business, trade or farming]? Can a person claim to be a Shudra if he abandons service to the higher three classes?

"There is no physical difference between human beings as there is between cows and horses. Actually, all living beings should be treated with respect, knowing that they are one in quality as spirit souls, although they may temporarily have different varieties of forms and activities." (BP, 38.33-34)

"Therefore, the caste system in human society that is based solely upon birth should be understood as superficial, because it is not prescribed in the scriptures. Unfortunately, those in ignorance cannot understand that it is a man-made concoction that can be easily refuted by a person in knowledge." (BP, 38.35)

"If a person considers himself to be a Brahmana by birth but engages in [such things as] taking care of cows, buffalos, goats, horses, camels, or sheep, or acts as a messenger, tax collector, businessman, painter [artist], or dancer, he should be considered as not a real Brahmana, even though he may be very expert or powerful." (BP, 38.36-37)

"Brahmanas who have deviated from the path of righteousness as propagated by the scriptures are to be considered fallen [from their social status], even though they may belong to a very aristocratic family, and have performed all the required purificatory rituals, and carefully studied the *Vedas*. No amount of accomplishments gives one the right to justify sinful behavior." (BP, 38.42-43)

"Thus, it can be understood how a Brahmana can become a Shudra, a Shudra can become a Brahmana, a Kshatriya can become a Brahmana or a Vaishya, and so on." (BP, 38.47)

Herein we can understand that a Brahmana is no Brahmana if he is not endowed with purity and good character, or if he leads a life of frivolity and immorality. However, a Shudra is a Brahmana if he leads a virtuous and pious life. Varna or caste is a question of character. Varna is not the color of the skin, but the color of one's character and quality. Conduct and character is what matters and not lineage alone. If one is Brahmana by birth and, at the same time, if he possesses the virtues of a Brahmana, that it is extremely good, because it is only certain virtuous qualifications that determine if one is a Brahmana, just as certain qualities distinguish one as a Kshatriya, Vaishya or Shudra. But if a Brahmana does not have the necessary traits, then he cannot call himself a Brahmana.

"Brahma said: If study of the *Vedas* is an important criteria for being recognized as a Brahmana, then many Kshatriyas and Vaisyas also deserve to be called Brahmanas, just as Ravana [who was born a Brahmana] became known as a demon [by qualities and actions]. Similarly, there are many dog-eaters, laborers, hunters, fishermen, sailors, and other people [outside the higher classes] who study the *Vedas*... Therefore, mere study of the *Vedas* cannot be the criteria for determining a person's social position." (BP, 39.1-2, 6)

The point is that "One who is twice-born [initiated through purificatory processes] and has thoroughly studied the *Vedas*, along with its six branches, cannot claim to be a purified soul if he does not observe the codes of good conduct. It is the occupational duty of one who is twice-born to study the *Vedas*, and this is one of the symptoms of a genuine Brahmana. If a person does not perform his prescribed duties after studying the four *Vedas*, he is like a eunuch who cannot take advantage of having a wife." (BP, 39.8-9)

Here again we see that the proper classification of an individual is not the status of one's birth family, but the qualities that he shows in life. Otherwise, even someone who considers himself to be a sophisticated Brahmana may indeed be something far less. As it is further explained: "Just like a Brahmana, a Shudra can have a *shikha* [tuft of hair on a shaved head], chant Om, worship the deities every morning and evening, wear a sacred thread [for chanting gayatri], carry a staff, and wear a deerskin [like a forest sage]. Even Brahma, Vishnu and Shiva are incapable of preventing people from becoming Shudras, and so what to speak of human beings. Therefore, wearing a sacred thread, keeping a *shikha*, and dressing a particular way are not really indications of a person's position within the varnashrama society. Who can stop a person's Shudra mentality, even though he may be well-versed in the Vedic mantras and tantras, and is a very good speaker on these subjects?" (BP, 39.10-13)

"[Generally it can be recognized that] All classes of men are seen to be capable of performing austerities, speaking the truth, worshiping the demigods, and chanting mantras. All classes of men generally avoid and [in some cases] even deceive those who speak harshly. Considering this, it is not possible to actually differentiate between a Brahmana and a Shudra. The power to curse and the exhibition of compassion can also be found in Shudras. One cannot ascertain from a person's external appearance whether he is a thief, a cheater, or a prince. Just as a Shudra is incapable of relieving himself of his miseries and protecting his family, it is the same for a Brahmana." (BP, 39.14-17)

THE DAMAGE OF UNQUALIFIED BRAHMANAS

"It is better if there are no Brahmanas at all than to have sinful and unqualified Brahmanas in the kingdom [who thus mislead society by what they say and do], especially in Kali-yuga, because in previous ages such Brahmanas would have been censored." (BP, 39.18)

Furthermore, it is especially difficult in these days to find anyone who is eligible to be considered a member of the higher classes or varnas of society, for it seems that everyone is materially motivated.

"According to some opinion, the power to curse others, a compassionate nature, and an inclination toward spiritual life are the characteristics of a Brahmana. In spite of that, it is seen that practically everyone is attached to worldly activities, having fallen into the darkness of ignorance, and because of that they are helplessly rushing towards hell, just like flies rush towards a fire." (BP, 39.19-20)

SO WHO IS A REAL BRAHMANA?

We have now seen by the logic presented in the *Bhavishya Purana* how the *jati* or birth of an individual does not justify anyone's social classification. But also how many of those who take pride in considering themselves of a higher caste or varna are actually not qualified in such a way at all? And yet, even a low-class person, meaning having taken birth from a lower social class, can indeed change to be a Brahmama. It all depends on one's level of consciousness, which generally depends on one's training and then mental disposition towards a spiritual life, and his natural inclination to follow a code of good conduct.

"Only those who have been PROPERLY trained and who have studied the *Vedas* [are seen to generally] adhere to a life of piety, whereas those without training [in at least general moral standards], who have not studied the *Vedas* [nor their spiritual conclusion] engage in sinful activities. Because study of the *Vedas* is the primary duty of a Brahmana [or one who is seriously on the path to spiritual progress, thus showing Brahminical qualities], one who does not study the *Vedas* cannot be considered a genuine Brahmana." (BP, 39.25-26)

This is interesting because how many times have we met people who feel they have duly studied the Vedic conclusions but have yet to know how to apply them, nor have they continued to follow them, giving any number of excuses for their present activities. The above verses make it clear that one has to continue to follow the standards, and if he cannot, then he is no longer to be accepted as a person of a higher social class. And this can go for anyone and anywhere. If they have little respect for others, engage in materialistic pursuits without higher moral standards, then that person is someone with a low consciousness, or low varna.

A BRAHMANA CAN EASILY FALL DOWN, WHILE A SHUDRA CAN EASILY MOVE FORWARD

"A Brahmana can easily be diverted from his brahminical qualities and codes of good conduct if he becomes bewildered by desires for material enjoyment and blinded by pride, just like an ordinary materialistic person. Of course, anyone becomes degraded and goes to hell if he has a sinful nature, even after undergoing the *samskaras* [purificatory rites]. On the other hand, those who observe proper etiquette, even though they might not have undergone the *samskaras*, should be considered as Brahmanas.

"It is a fact that even someone who chants various mantras and has undergone all the purificatory rituals may fall down into illusion and thereby become bereft of brahminical qualifications due to his sinful mentality. People who engage in abominable activities, and who are blinded by pride in their ability, fall down from their position and lose all brahminical qualities." (BP, 40.15-18)

Here again I am reminded of what I have always said, that the present caste system based on one's *jati* or birth is unjust. It is meant to depend on the person's natural talents, abilities, tendencies, and mentality, which varies from person to person regardless of family, social class, culture, regional jurisdiction, etc. Each person has to be considered individually regardless of family background.

"The caste system based simply on birth does not actually divide people according to their development of consciousness. It is one's envy and hatred that allows us to place a person in a higher or lower category. If it is not helpful to divide people according to their bodily characteristics, [then why do so]? In the past, many great sages, such as Srila Vyasadeva, observed proper etiquette and became great souls, although they did not undergo the *samskaras*, such as the *garbhadhana*." (BP, 40.19-20)

For example, "Vyasadeva was the son of a fisherman's daughter, his father Parashara was born from a woman who was a dog-eater. Shukadeva was born from a female parrot, Vashishtha was the son of a prostitute..." and other sages like Kanada, Shringi, Mandapala, and Mandavya all had questionable births, and yet all were highly qualified Brahmanas, and recognized as such.

"Indeed, it is imperative that one strictly follow the instructions of these highly qualified sages, who all possess a spotless character, if one hopes to achieve success in life.

"O King, undergoing the various *samskaras* certainly plays an important part in raising one to the platform of a qualified Brahmana, but there are many other important considerations. For example, the great sage Shringi achieved the status of a Brahmana on the strength of his austerities. It must be concluded that undergoing *samskaras* is a principal criteria for becoming a Brahmana. Still, on the strength of their penance and austerity, Vyasadeva, Parashara, Kanada,

Vashishtha, and Mandapala became qualified Brahmanas, despite their taking birth from the womb of a fisherwomen, female dog-eater, or prostitute, etc.

"[Therefore] undergoing the various *samskaras* is not sufficient to qualify one as a Brahmana. Those who are expert in performing the Vedic and tantrik *samskaras* require the attainment of transcendental knowledge and the performance of penance to support their claim of being qualified Brahmanas. Without such qualifications, one will certainly indulge in sinful activities and thus fall from his high position as a Brahmana. One who is a Brahmana in name only is not really a Brahmana." (BP, 40.22-32)

Here in these quotations we can see that many great Rishis were born in lower varnas, such as Vashishta was the son of a prostitute; Vyasa was born of a fisher woman; Parashara's mother was a chandala; Nammalwar was a Shudra. Similarly, Valmiki, Viswamitra, Agastya were Brahmanas in spite of their non-Brahmana origin. All this proves that birth is not a major player in attaining the status of Brahmana. It is the intellectual and spiritual level of consciousness that differentiates people.

In the same way, spiritual realization is not dependent on birth or book-learning, as has been repeatedly demonstrated in the lives of saints, from the very earliest times to our own day. So, then who is a real rishi? It is the person who has attained through proper means the direct realization of Dharma. That is the one who can be a rishi even if he is a non-Brahmana or a mleccha [outcaste] by birth.

The basis of varna is *guna* or the mode of nature in which a person is situated, and not birth. Therefore, one is a Brahmana not because of one's birth or caste or heredity or color or profession or acquisition of worldly knowledge, or mere observation of social and moral codes, but because of his spiritual knowledge and insight, and his abidance in the Supreme Reality, his state of self-realization. This is the conclusion of all *Vedas, Shrutis, Puranas, Itihasas*, and of all great men of India.

Therefore, casteism, meaning judging a person by one's birth family, is a misguided social custom and not part of any spiritual tradition, and all our great preachers have tried to break it down. From Buddhism downwards, every sect has preached against caste.

WHEN A BRAHMANA BECOMES
LOWER THAN A SHUDRA

"According to Svayambhuva Manu, the principal characteristic of a Brahmana is that he possesses spiritual knowledge, is enriched with the power of penance, and maintains a state of purity. According to this understanding, anyone, whether he belongs to an upper, middle, or lower caste, if he never indulges in sinful activities, he must be considered a Brahmana. It is said that an honest and well-behaved Shudra is better than an arrogant Brahmana, and a Brahmana who disregards the prescribed codes of good conduct is inferior to a Shudra. A Shudra that does not keep wine in his shop or in his house is called an honest Shudra." (BP, 42.29-32)

HOW EVERYONE CAN ADVANCE

The proper observance of the Vedic system of varnashrama-dharma is to help one's growth and self-development. The great sages have explained that this system of dividing society into varnas is the stepping-stone to civilization, providing a means so one can rise higher and higher in proportion to one's learning and culture. Such is our ideal for raising all humanity slowly and gently towards the realization of the great ideal of being a spiritual man, who is calm, steady, worshipful, pure, and meditative. In that ideal there is God-realization.

The additional aim of varnashrama-dharma is to promote the development of the universal, eternal Sanatana-dharma, the balanced state of being in which you perceive and live according to your genuine spiritual identity. This is the ultimate goal of the whole Vedic system for all of humanity. Thus, as the saying goes, "if you take care of Dharma, Dharma will take care of you." If you destroy it, society will become bereft of balance. Therefore, we should never destroy our Dharma. This principle holds true of the individual as much as of the nation. It is Dharma alone which keeps a nation alive and moving forward. Dharma is the very soul of man. Dharma is the very soul of a nation also, even the world. So how can we all move forward together on the sure path of progress? Here it is explained as follows:

"Brahminical prowess progressively increases in pious persons who cultivate godly qualities such as forgiveness, control of the senses, compassion, charity, truthfulness, purity, meditation, respect for others, simplicity, satisfaction, freedom from false ego, austerity, self-control, knowledge, freedom from the propensity to blaspheme others, celibacy, cultivation of knowledge, freedom from envy, faithfulness, freedom from hatred, detachment, renunciation of the thirst for material enjoyment, service to the spiritual master, and control of the body, mind, and speech." (BP, 42.12-15)

"Many persons in the past became highly advanced and powerful by cultivating these qualities and practicing behavior befitting a saintly person. It is a fact that by such a practice, the heart becomes purified, freeing one from the influence of the modes of passion [raja-guna] and ignorance [tamo-guna]." (BP, 42.16)

"According to learned authorities, those who possess these godly qualities are actually scholars of the Vedas and Puranas, and understand the confidential purport of the Bhagavad-gita. By faithfully following the principles of varna and *ashrama*, people in all four yugas [from Satya-yuga to Kali-yuga] have attained the perfection of life." (BP, 42.17-18)

CLASSIFICATIONS BASED ON THE BODY ARE COMPLETELY FALSE

By now we should be able to see that even a person who has taken birth from a family who has been considered of a low varna can raise him or herself up to a higher classification by having proper training and showing appropriate codes of conduct and lifestyle.

"When a Shudra has become advanced by undergoing the [Vedic] *samskaras*, he can no longer be considered a Shudra. The conclusion is that a person's external dress or appearance cannot be the criterion for his being accepted as a Brahmana." (BP, 39.29)

However, the *samskaras* or rituals and training in themselves cannot be the sole means of determining one's social position. This certainly helps, but there must be more than that, which, is already explained.

"If the undergoing of *samskaras* is the main criteria for being accepted as a Brahmana, then all those who have undergone *samskaras* are certainly Brahmanas. If that be the case, how can they be compared with personalities like Srila Vyasadeva, who did not undergo the *samskaras*. If we consider this, we see that there is no support for the theory of different varnas. Although different varnas are recognized in society, this is just an artificial conception of materialistic people. The material body is composed of the five gross elements—earth, water, fire, air, and sky. These elements cannot be the cause for one being accepted as a Brahmana [or anything else], because they combine for some time and then merge back into their source. Indeed, the body of an atheist, mleccha, or a yavana is made of the same material elements.

[Thus, such designations based on the body are completely false]." (BP, 39.30-33)

"Religiosity as described in the *Vedas* can also be found in people who are sinful, violent, of bad character, and cruel. Therefore the determination of one's social status does not depend on undergoing [purificatory] *samskaras*." (BP, 39.34)

"Therefore, [from the conclusions that have been presented so far] there is no difference between a Brahmana and a Shudra in terms of bodily features, mentality, experience of happiness and distress, opulence, prowess, tendency toward gambling, shrewdness in business, ability to earn wealth, steadiness, restlessness, intelligence, detachment, virtue, accomplishment of the three objectives of life [*dharma, artha* and *kama*], cleverness, beauty, complexion, sexual capacity, stool, bones, holes of the body, manifestations of love, height, weight, and bodily hair. Therefore, even if the demigods were to try very hard to find distinctions between Brahmanas and Shudras [and everyone in between] in this way, they would not be able to do so." (BP, 39.35-39)

"One should not think that all Brahmanas are white like moon rays, that all Kshatriyas have a complexion like the color of a kimsuka flower, that all Vaishyas have a golden complexion like the color of an orpiment fruit, and that all Shudras are black like half-burnt coal. How can there be four classes of human beings when their walking, complexion, hair, happiness, distress, blood, skin, flesh, bone marrow, and fluids are totally identical? There is nothing special about anyone's complexion, height, weight, figure, period of stay within the womb, speech, wisdom, working senses, life-air, strength, illnesses, objectives of life, and methods for curing diseases." (BP, 39.41-43)

"A father may have four sons and it is assumed that all of them belong to the same varna as their father. Similarly, all living entities are produced by the one Supreme Father and so, how can His children be divided into different varnas? Just as the color, texture, structure, feel, and juice of different portions of a fig are the same, so are the human beings that are emanating from one source, and so it is improper to differentiate between them. The brothers, children, daughters-in-law, births, marriages, beauty, complexion, and artistic ability must be the same for the member of the lineages [or *gotras*] coming from Kaushika, Gautama, Kaumdinya, Mandavya, Vashishtha, Atreya, Kautsa, Angirasa, Maudgalya, Katyayana, and Bhargava.

"Although some learned scholars accept the material body as being a Brahmana [or something else], this indicates that they are in the bodily concept of life [without spiritual perception], which exists in a condition of dense ignorance. This is like a blind person desiring to treat others' eyes by applying a black ointment. Both are ludicrous. Because the material body has a beginning, it also has an end. After death, the elements of the body merge into the totality of material elements once again. Therefore, the body [alone] cannot be accepted as a Brahmana [or any other varna]." (BP, 39.45-51)

In conclusion, therefore, "Only ignorant people accept this material body as being a Brahmana [or any other varna]. According to their understanding, the position of being a Brahmana cannot be achieved simply by undergoing the various purificatory processes." (BP, 39.54)

ONE MISSES GOAL OF LIFE
WHEN PREOCCUPIED BY CASTE

"If after attaining the human form of life, which enables one to possess things like attractive bodily features, abundant wealth, great power and prestige, one does not live according to the prescribed religious principles, it cannot be predicted what species of life he will thereafter be forced to accept on various planets. This is the fate of one who is so proud that he dares to challenge the supremacy of God. Being intoxicated by pride, thinking that their caste, race, beauty, social status, and education are very wonderful, people do not bother to understand their actual self-interest, and because of that in their next life they will suffer like eunuchs.

"Material existence can be compared to a huge pit in which thousands of millions of living entities are drowning. Knowing this perfectly well, which intelligent person would be very proud of his caste [varna]?

"There are many human beings who are presumed to be fully satisfied, having been born in aristocratic families, and yet because of their own misdeeds, after death they will be forced to take birth in this world in some lower species of life. In this world, no one can remain permanently in some situation." (BP, 39.3-6)

If this does not make it clear regarding the impermanent nature of the bodily situation of the living being, and that even one's high, intermediate or low birth is temporary, then I do not know what can. Yet, we see that so many people are going through life, completely asleep in regard to the real purpose of this existence. Thus, they may think their present position is so grand, not knowing that if they do not use this life properly for real spiritual progress, after death their next life may not be very great at all. But how many lifetimes must we go through this before we learn our lessons about the real truth of the matter, that our real position is as a spiritual being, beyond the body and its superficial designations, and everything else is temporary and secondary?

THE DIFFERENCE OF PROPER CONSCIOUSNESS AND INTENT, OR MERELY GOING THROUGH THE MOTIONS

In the next few verses it is pointed out that a person must also have the proper concentration and focus, along with the proper intentions in their actions if they are expected to be qualified in their positions. Otherwise, it is seen that anyone can chant mantras and do rituals, but merely going through the motions, especially for adoration, profit and distinction, is not what is needed to suitably accept or be qualified for a higher status in one's social classification.

"Generally, those who are twice-born—the Brahmanas, Kshatriyas, and Vaishyas—undergo all the Vedic *samskaras*. For this reason, they are certainly to be considered as superior to the Shudras who engage in all kinds of frivolous activities.

"In spite of undergoing the *samskaras*, if those who are twice-born engage in violent and sinful activities, such as killing a Brahmana [or worse], having sexual intercourse with the wife of the spiritual master, stealing, killing a cow, drinking wine, cheating, speaking lies, exhibiting great pride, speaking atheistic philosophy, blaspheming the *Vedas*, denying the authority of the *Vedas*, plundering the wealth of others, acting whimsically, earning money by dancing or cheating, eating all types of abominable food, and performing any other prohibited activity with the body, mind, and speech, they can never be considered purified, even if they perform thousands of sacrifices [rituals].

"Therefore, the ability to chant mantras, perform fire rituals, practice penance, and sacrifices does not make one a Brahmana, just as a Shudra remains a Shudra, despite the ability to perform all these activities [when merely going through the motions]." (BP, 41.5-9)

"Similarly, the Brahmanas who indulge in sinful activities must be considered fallen. Therefore, the only sane conclusion is that the concepts of Brahmana and Kshatriya, etc., are temporary designations and not ultimate reality." (BP, 41.52)

EXPECTED CHARACTERISTICS AND ACTIONS
OF EACH PERSON OF THE FOUR VARNAS

What follows are a very few of the qualities, actions and characteristics that are typical of people in each of the four varnas. This is simply to make the characteristics a little more clear.

"Brahma said: Genuine Brahmanas know very well what is to be accepted and what is to be rejected. They avoid sinful behavior, carefully control their senses, mind, and speech, and carefully observe the prescribed etiquette. They follow the rules and regulations that are prescribed for them in the scriptures, and constantly work for the welfare of others. They work for the protection of religious principles in this world and are fixed in trance, meditating on the Absolute Truth. They restrain their anger, and are free from material attachment, envy, lamentation, and pride. They are attached to the study of the *Vedas* [and their supporting literature], very peaceful, and are the best well-wishing friends of all living entities. They are equal in happiness and distress, reside in a solitary place, observe all the vows prescribed for them with their body and mind, and are pious by nature. They are reluctant to perform any abominable act, and are freed from illusion and false pride. They are charitable, compassionate, truthful, and very learned in the scriptures. They know the Supreme Brahman and have high regard for the revealed scriptures." (BP, 42.1-7)

From this verse we can understand that if a Brahmana is not free from such things as anger, material attachment, envy, lamentation, and pride, along with the other qualities mentioned above, then such people do not have the real mentality of a Brahmana, even if they do appear to have some expertise in other areas, or are born in a Brahmana family. Thus, they are not genuinely qualified to be spiritual authorities for the rest of society, but, indeed, have much more work to do on themselves for their own progress and development.

Another class of beings are also known as Brahmanas, as explained: "Brahma was born from the navel of the *purusha-avatara* [Vishnu]. All living entities were manifested by Him, and among them, those who are devotees, surrendered souls unto that Supreme Personality of Godhead, are also known as Brahmanas." (BP, 42.9)

Furthermore, "Those who have some realization of the Supreme Brahman, and who act according to the prescribed codes of good conduct, are called Brahmanas, and they are glorified by the other members of society." (BP, 42.11)

In regard to the other main varnas, namely the Kshatriyas, Vaishyas, and Shudras, their expected standards are also briefly described: "Those who give protection to others, saving them from all kinds of danger, are known as Kshatriyas. Those who engage in farming, cow protection, and trading are known as Vaishyas, and those who have no capacity to study the *Vedas* [or deep spiritual knowledge], and are engaged in serving members of the higher three classes are known as Shudras." (BP, 42.10)

"Lord Brahma has prescribed the methods for members of all the varnas that will enable them to achieve perfection by performing their respective duties.

"Among the human beings, those who are comparatively more powerful and are thus able to give protection to others, saving them from all types of danger, should be known as Kshatriyas. Persons who approach the Kshatriyas to beg some charity after instructing them on the messages of the Supreme Lord as found in the Vedic literature should be known as Brahmanas.

"Those who are almost as powerful as the Kshatriyas but engage in agriculture, cow protection, and trade [such as banking and business], should be known as Vaishyas. Those who, not very capable of working independently, and who are easily overcome by lamentation and illusion, should engage in the service of the higher three classes of men and thus be known as Shudras. In this way, according to their nature and qualities, there are prescribed duties for Brahmanas, Kshatriyas, Vaishyas, and Shudras." (BP, 42.19-24)

"The qualities of a Brahmana are peacefulness, austerity, self-control, purity, tolerance, simplicity, knowledge, the practical application of the knowledge, and inquiry into the nature of the Absolute Truth. Heroism, power, determination, resourcefulness, courage in battle, generosity and leadership are the natural qualities of work for the Kshatriyas. Farming, cow protection and business are the natural work for the Vaishyas, and for the Shudras there is labor and service to others." (BP, 42.25-27)

In this way, everyone has a natural tendency for some aspect of the particular traits described, and are also a part of the social body of civilization to help contribute to its balance and progress, and the well-being of one and all.

IN CONCLUSION

If people can understand the real basis of the varna system, and be trained in acting accordingly, raising themselves to their original spiritual level, then the false, superficial and bodily based sectarian spirit can ultimately be put to rest. Then there is every possibility that such people can develop a spiritual vision of one another with a mood of love, care, cooperation, sacrifice, and service. This is the real purpose of the varnashrama system anyway, to see that everyone is a part of the larger social body, and part of the Supreme, and that each person, by their actions and occupation, has a contribution to make to the well-being of all. If people actually understood this and saw society in this way, it would tend to nullify what is called caste-based discrimination, which has been part of the misunderstanding and misapplication of what is called the caste system that we find today, which was not a part of the traditional Vedic varnashrama system.

"It is therefore to be concluded that humanity is essentially one, but distinctions of caste [varnas] have been made according to a person's qualities and work [mentality and consciousness]. As far as general behavior is concerned, the entire human race is one. There is only a difference in people's occupations and attitudes. Those who divide society into castes according to birth cannot see that human beings are essentially one." (BP, 42.33-34)

CHAPTER THREE

Determining Our Varna by The Modes of Nature (Gunas) in Which We are Situated

In the last chapter, the whole idea of one's varna or social qualification is determined by the person's qualities. It is the intention, tendencies, interests, talents, and proclivities that ultimately determine one's place in society, which includes one's career and occupational abilities, and where a person would be most productive and contributing to society, and thus also, most happy and satisfied. This is the ultimate purpose of revealing one's varna, which, as previously explained, is often determined while one is a youth, as recognized by qualified counselors through tests or observations of the child's habits and interests and abilities, and by seeing in which *gunas* or modes of nature a child or person operates. Which *gunas* or modes of nature with which we associate can also be determined by an understanding of the analysis as outlined in the following description, which is taken primarily from the *Bhagavad-gita*.

To begin with, as we previously mentioned, there are three modes, called *gunas*. One is the mode of goodness, *sattva-guna*; one is the mode of passion, *raja-guna*; and the other is the mode of ignorance or darkness, called *tama-guna*.

By understanding the modes of nature, we can realize in which mode we are primarily situated and, thus, determine what our consciousness is and which varna we are most likely to belong to, and even what our next existence after this life is likely to be.

WHAT ARE THE MODES OF NATURE

First of all, let us understand that no one in the material atmosphere is free from the modes of nature, as stated in *Bhagavad-gita*: "There is no being existing, either here or among the demigods in the higher planetary systems, which is freed from the three modes of material nature." (*Bg.*18.40)

These material modes manifest within one's mind and are always in competition with each other. According to a person's activities, we can understand his state of mind as well as by which particular mode he is being influenced. "Material nature consists of the three modes--goodness, passion and ignorance. When the living entity comes in contact with nature, he becomes conditioned by these modes. The mode of goodness, being purer than the others, is illuminating, and it frees one from all sinful reactions. Those situated in that mode develop knowledge, but they become conditioned by the concept of happiness. The mode of passion is born of unlimited desires and longings, and because of this one is bound to material fruitive activities. The mode of ignorance causes the delusion of all living entities. The result of this mode is madness, indolence, and sleep, which bind the conditioned soul. Sometimes the mode of passion becomes prominent, defeating the mode of goodness. And sometimes the mode of goodness defeats passion, and other times the mode of ignorance defeats goodness and passion. In this way, there is always competition for supremacy." (*Bg.*14.5-8,10)

From this description, we can begin to recognize the fact that the mind, which is the center of our senses and an instrument that operates on the material platform, is what creates the illusion of our material happiness and distress due to the influence of the modes of nature. As stated in *Srimad-Bhagavatam*: "Rather, it is the mind alone that causes happiness and distress and perpetuates the rotation of material life. The powerful mind actuates the functions of the material modes, from which evolve the different kinds of material activities in the modes of goodness, ignorance, and passion. From the activities in each of these modes develop the corresponding statuses [one's position or varna] of life." (*Bhag.*11.23.42-43)

What this means is that by embracing the mind and body as being our real identity, we become subjected to the control of the modes of material nature. From this, we are practically forced to engage in the struggle of trying to attain our likes and avoid our dislikes. This is the materialistic occupation of the living entity which makes a person work or act in a certain way, and manifest the person's many interests, attractions, and develop the plans to attain them. It is this combination of karma and *gunas* in which the person associates that help determine the kind of varna or occupation or social status for which the person is most suited. Whatever material activity we decide to engage in is our choice of which mode or combination of modes with which we will associate. It is this choice which determines our status not only in this life, but how we attain our position or condition in the next life.

In the material world, we think we are free to choose what we will do, but our freedom is also a matter of choosing which combination of material modes with which we will relate. Therefore, due to the mode of goodness, someone may become a clean and healthy person, searching for higher aspects of life. Due to the mode of passion, a person may become a workaholic, desiring to achieve fame, fortune, and distinction. Due to the mode of ignorance, another person may become a lazy drunkard who simply feels sorry for himself for not attaining the success which he feels life owes him. In this way, we create our destiny and are forced to face the consequences of the choices we make depending on the modes with which we decide to associate.

Real free will means to be free from the binding forces of the modes of material nature which affect the way we see things and how we make our choices through life. We, therefore, must understand how the modes work, how to recognize their influence on us, and the process to get free from them.

HOW THE MODES OF NATURE WORK

Besides affecting the individual, the modes also have particular influences over the whole universe. The Vedic literature establishes that during the creation of the material world the time element agitates the modes, which, thus, produces past, present, and future, or the creation, maintenance, and annihilation of the world. This is explained as follows: "Nature exists originally as the equilibrium of the three material modes, which pertain only to nature, not to the transcendental spirit soul. These modes--goodness, passion, and ignorance--are the effective causes of the creation, maintenance, and destruction of this universe. In this world the mode of goodness is recognized as knowledge, the mode of passion as fruitive work, and the mode of darkness as ignorance. Time is perceived as the agitated interaction of the material modes, and the totality of functional propensity is embodied by the primeval *sutra* or *mahat tattva* (total material energy)." (*Bhag.*11.22.12-13)

The effects that the modes have can also be seen through the unfolding of history. "With the increase of the mode of goodness, the strength of the demigods similarly increases. When passion increases, the demoniac become strong. And with the rise of ignorance, O Uddhava, the strength of the most wicked increases." (*Bhag.*11.25.19) Therefore, just as a change of wind direction brings a change of weather, time brings changes in the influence of the modes of nature, causing various types of people, civilizations, countries, ideas, or styles of art and music, etc., to become at first dominant in society and to again recede. What was popular and acceptable at one time, may be the reverse later on because of a change in the predominating modes of nature by which people are affected.

Whatever we are inclined to do on a material or bodily basis can be recognized as the effects of interacting with the modes. This is pointed out in *Srimad-Bhagavatam* (11.25.30-31): "Therefore, material substance, place, result of activity, time, knowledge, work, the performer of work, faith, state of consciousness, species of life and destination after death are all based on the three modes of material nature. O best of human beings, all states of material being are related to the interaction of the enjoying soul and material nature. Whether seen, heard of, or only conceived within the mind, they are without exception constituted of the modes of nature."

To recognize the modes and how they influence us, further elaboration is given in *Srimad-Bhagavatam* (11.25.2-18): "Mind and sense control, tolerance, discrimination, sticking to one's prescribed duty, truthfulness, mercy, careful study of the past and future, satisfaction in any condition, generosity, renunciation of sense gratification, faith in the spiritual master, being embarrassed at improper action, charity, simplicity, humbleness, and satisfaction within oneself are qualities of the mode of goodness.

"Material desire, great endeavor, audacity, dissatisfaction even in gain, false pride, praying for material advancement, considering oneself different and better than others, sense gratification, rash eagerness to fight, a fondness for hearing oneself praised, the tendency to ridicule others, advertising one's own prowess, and justifying one's actions by one's strength are qualities of the mode of passion.

"Intolerant anger, stinginess, speaking without scriptural authority, violent hatred, living as a parasite, hypocrisy, chronic fatigue, quarrel, lamentation, delusion, unhappiness, depression, sleeping too much, false expectations, fear, and laziness constitute the major qualities of the mode of ignorance. Now please hear about the combination of these three modes.

"My dear Uddhava, the combination of all three modes is present in the mentality of 'I' and 'mine.' The ordinary transactions of this world, which are carried out through the agency of the mind, the objects of perception, the senses and the vital airs of the physical body, are also based on the combination of the modes. When a person devotes himself to religiosity, economic development and sense gratification, the faith, wealth, and sensual enjoyment obtained by his endeavors display the interaction of the three modes of nature. When a man desires sense gratification, being attached to family life, and when he consequently becomes established in religious and occupational duties, the combination of the modes of nature is manifest. A person exhibiting qualities such as self-control is understood to be predominantly in the mode of goodness. Similarly, a passionate person is recognized by his lust, and one in ignorance is recognized by qualities such as anger.

"Any person, whether man or woman, who worships Me [Sri Krishna] with loving devotion, offering his or her prescribed duties unto Me without material attachment, is understood to be situated in goodness. When a person worships Me by his prescribed duties with the hope of gaining material benefit, his nature should be understood to be in passion, and one who worships Me with the desire to commit violence against others is in ignorance.

"The three modes of material nature--goodness, passion and ignorance--influence the living entity but not Me. Manifesting within his mind, they induce the living entity to become attached to material bodies and other created objects. In this way, the living entity is bound up. When the mode of goodness, which is luminous, pure and auspicious, predominates over passion and ignorance, a man becomes endowed with happiness, virtue, knowledge, and other good qualities. When the mode of passion, which causes attachment, separation and activity, conquers ignorance and goodness, a man begins to work hard to acquire prestige and fortune. Thus, in the mode of passion he experiences anxiety and struggle. When the mode of ignorance conquers passion and goodness, it covers one's consciousness and makes one foolish and dull. Falling into lamentation and illusion, a person in the mode of ignorance sleeps excessively, indulges in false hopes, and displays violence toward others.

"When consciousness becomes clear and the senses are detached from matter, one experiences fearlessness within the material body and detachment from the material mind. You should understand this situation to be the predominance of the mode of goodness, in which one has the opportunity to realize Me.

"You should discern the mode of passion by its symptoms--the distortion of the intelligence because of too much activity, the inability of the perceiving senses to disentangle themselves from mundane objects, an unhealthy condition of the working physical organs, and the unsteady perplexity of the mind.

"When one's higher awareness fails and finally disappears and one is thus unable to concentrate his attention, his mind is ruined and manifests ignorance and depression. You should understand this situation to be the predominance of the mode of ignorance."

By studying these explanations, we can distinguish by which mode we are being influenced, and then of which varna or occupation and career may be most suitable for us. We can also understand that the individual spirit soul is above the modes, but as long as one identifies with the mind, where the modes manifest, and remains on the material platform, one continues being controlled by the various combinations of these modes. This, along with one's past karma, is how one continues in the cycle of birth and death and remains attached to material activities. "Due to this external energy, the living entity, although transcendental to the three modes of material nature, thinks of himself as a material product and thus undergoes the reactions of material miseries." (*Bhag*.1.7.5)

Remember, one of the purposes of the varnashrama system is not only to help a person find the most suitable occupation and happiness in life, but to arrange life in a way that the person can progress spiritually throughout his or her life, and finally rise above these modes of nature and the system of varna and ashram altogether. This leads to a spiritual consciousness in the individual that then leads to liberation from the material world and entrance into the spiritual realm.

How we can more closely recognize the effects of the *gunas* or modes of material nature in various ways is further described as follows.

ACTION AND CONSCIOUSNESS IN VARIOUS MODES

By now you probably understand that our consciousness, viewpoint, attitude, desires, and the outcome of those all depend on how we interact with the modes of nature. By studying the following descriptions of the kind of work, faith, knowledge, sacrifices, austerities, food, and happiness that are found in the three modes of material nature, we can understand which of the modes affect us the most. Depending on which mode or combination of modes in which we are situated determines our whole outlook on life and the kind of results we can expect to attain. We can also analyze the activities of our friends to understand in which modes they are situated and what results are likely to take place in their lives, along with what affect their association is likely to have on us.

Action and Work

"As for actions, that action in accordance with duty, which is performed without attachment, without love or hate, by one who has renounced fruitive results, is called action in the mode of goodness. But action performed with great effort by one seeking to gratify his desires, and which is enacted from a sense of false ego, is called action in the mode of passion. And that action performed in ignorance and delusion without consideration of future bondage or consequences, which inflicts injury and is impractical, is said to be action in the mode of ignorance.

"The worker who is free from all material attachments and false ego, who is enthusiastic and resolute and who is indifferent to success or failure, is a worker in the mode of goodness. But that worker who is attached to the fruits of his labor and who passionately wants to enjoy them, who is greedy, envious and impure and moved by happiness and distress, is a worker in the mode of passion. And that worker who is always engaged in work against the injunction of the scripture, who is materialistic, obstinate, cheating and expert in insulting others, who is lazy, always morose and procrastinating, is a worker in the mode of ignorance." (*Bg*.18.23-28)

Residence

"Residence in the forest is in the mode of goodness, residence in a town is in the mode of passion, residence in a gambling house or [similar places such as bars, racetracks, brothels, etc.] displays the quality of ignorance, and residence in a place where I [the Supreme, or Deity of the Supreme] reside is transcendental." (*Bhag.*11.25.25)

Faith

"Faith directed toward spiritual life is in the mode of goodness, faith rooted in fruitive work is in the mode of passion, faith residing in irreligious activities is in the mode of ignorance, but faith in My devotional service is purely transcendental." (*Bhag.*11.25.27)

Understanding

"O son of Pritha, that understanding by which one knows what ought to be done and what ought not to be done, what is feared and what is not to be feared, what is binding and what is liberating, that understanding is established in the mode of goodness. And that understanding which cannot distinguish between the religious way of life and the irreligious, between action that should be done and action that should not be done, that imperfect understanding is in the mode of passion. That understanding which considers irreligion to be religion and religion to be irreligion, under the spell of illusion and darkness, and strives always in the wrong direction is in the mode of ignorance." (*Bg.*18.30-32)

Knowledge

"That knowledge by which one undivided spiritual nature is seen in all existences, undivided and divided, is knowledge in the mode of goodness. That knowledge by which a different type of living entity is seen to be dwelling in different bodies is knowledge in the mode of passion. And that knowledge by which one is attached to one kind of work as the all in all, without knowledge of the truth, and which is very meager, is said to be in the mode of darkness." (*Bg.*18.20-22)

Sacrifices

"Of sacrifices, that sacrifice performed according to duty and to scriptural rules, and with no expectation of reward, is of the nature of goodness. But that sacrifice performed for some material end or benefit or performed ostentatiously, out of pride, is of the nature of passion. And that sacrifice performed in defiance of scriptural injunctions, in which no spiritual food is distributed, no hymns are chanted and no remunerations are made to the priests, and which is faithless--that sacrifice is of the nature of ignorance." (*Bg.* 17.11-13)

Austerities

"The austerity of the body consists in this: worship of the Supreme Lord, the brahmanas, the spiritual master, and superiors like the father and mother. Cleanliness, simplicity, celibacy, and nonviolence are also austerities of the body. Austerity of speech consists in speaking truthfully and beneficially and in avoiding speech that offends. One should also recite the *Vedas* regularly. And serenity, simplicity, gravity, self-control, and purity of thought are the austerities of the mind. This threefold austerity, practiced by men whose aim is not to benefit themselves materially but to please the Supreme, is of the nature of goodness. Those ostentatious penances and austerities which are performed in order to gain respect, honor and reverence are said to be in the mode of passion. They are neither stable nor permanent. And those penances and austerities which are performed foolishly by means of obstinate self-torture, or to destroy or injure others, are said to be in the mode of ignorance." (*Bg.* 17.14-19)

Charity

"The gift which is given out of duty, at the proper time and place, to a worthy person, and without expectation of return is considered to be charity in the mode of goodness. But charity performed with the expectation of some return, or with a desire for fruitive results, or in a grudging mood, is said to be charity in the mode of passion. And charity performed at an improper place and time and given to unworthy persons without respect and with contempt is charity in the mode of ignorance." (*Bg.*17.20-22)

Foods

"Food that is wholesome, pure and obtained without difficulty is in the mode of goodness, food that gives immediate pleasure to the senses is in the mode of passion, and food that is unclean and causes distress is in the mode of ignorance." (*Bhag.*11.25.28)

"Foods in the mode of goodness increase the duration of life, purify one's existence and give strength, health, happiness, and satisfaction. Such nourishing foods are sweet, juicy, fattening, and palatable. Foods that are too bitter, too sour, salty, pungent, dry, and hot, are liked by people in the modes of passion. Such foods cause pain, distress and disease. Food cooked more than three hours before being eaten, which is tasteless, stale, putrid, decomposed, and unclean, is food liked by people in the mode of ignorance." (*Bg.*17.8-10)

Happiness

"Now please hear from Me about the three kinds of happiness which the conditioned soul enjoys, and by which he sometimes comes to the end of all distress. That which in the beginning may be just like poison but at the end is just like nectar and which awakens one to self-realization is said to be happiness in the mode of goodness." (*Bg.*18.36-37)

This refers to happiness in connection with spiritual practices which may not always seem like they cater to the pleasure of the senses, for which our mind is always craving. Following rules and regulations for spiritual advancement sometimes appears difficult. But as we become more advanced, our taste for spiritual practices increases and the happiness found therein becomes unlimited. Whereas the happiness found in enjoying our senses seems very pleasurable at first, in the end, after repeating such acts many times, it becomes distasteful, as confirmed in the following verse:

"That happiness which is derived from contact of the senses with their objects and which appears like nectar at first but poison at the end is said to be of the nature of passion. And that happiness which is blind to self-realization, which is delusion from beginning to end and which arises from sleep, laziness and illusion is said to be of the nature of ignorance." (*Bg.*18.38-39)

"Happiness derived from the self is in the mode of goodness, happiness based on sense gratification is in the mode of passion, and happiness based on delusion and degradation is in the mode of ignorance. But that happiness found within Me is transcendental." (*Bhag.*11.25.29)

The following verses from the *Manu-samhita* further elaborate on which activities reflect the qualities of particular modes:

"When a man having done, doing or being about to do any act, feels ashamed, the learned may know that all such acts bear the mark of the quality of Darkness (ignorance)." (*Manu.*12.35)

This kind of act also depends on one's conscience. If a person has no moral training, then he may do anything and never feel any shame or remorse. If such is the case, we can understand that his consciousness is in the mode of ignorance, like that of an animal.

"But when a man desires to gain by an act much fame in this world and feels no sorrow on failing, know that it bears the mark of the quality of Activity (passion). But that bears the mark of the quality of Goodness which with his whole heart he desires to know, which he is not ashamed to perform, and at which his soul rejoices. The craving after sensual pleasures is to be the mark of Darkness, the pursuit of wealth the mark of Activity, and the desire to gain spiritual merit the mark of Goodness; each later named quality is better than the preceding one." (*Manu*.12.36-38)

WHERE THE MODES TAKE US

After reading the descriptions of how the modes of material nature work and affect us, and in which of the modes various activities are situated, it is now time to find out what our destination is by associating with these modes.

The point is that by performing various material activities that are closely linked to the modes of nature, our consciousness and existence will develop accordingly. For example, as the *Bhagavad-gita* explains: "The manifestations of the mode of goodness can be experienced when all the gates of the body are illuminated by knowledge. When there is an increase in the mode of passion, the symptoms of great attachment, uncontrollable desire, hankering, and intense endeavor develop. When there is an increase in the mode of ignorance, madness, illusion, inertia, and darkness are manifested." (*Bg.* 14.11-13)

How we can begin to increase or decrease the effects the modes of nature have on us can be understood by studying the previous descriptions of actions in the modes and then adjusting our lifestyle accordingly. For instance, if we live in a hotel with a bar and topless nightclub, and eat food that has been cooked by low-class and unclean people, and drink liquor and spend our time gambling and going through the emotions of anger, attachment, lamentation, moroseness, etc., as we win or lose at the betting games, then this will submerge us deep into the mode of ignorance. Thus, we will be obliged to suffer the necessary consequences of anxiety, disease, and short duration of life that accompany the lifestyle in that mode.

On the other hand, if we live a peaceful life in the country, breathing the fresh air and eating ripe fruits and vegetables, working only as necessary to maintain ourselves while engaged with proper faith and understanding in spiritual pursuits, then we will certainly be in the mode of goodness and experience the uplifting results. This is also pointed out in *Bhagavad-gita* (14.16): "By acting in the mode of goodness, one becomes purified. Works done in the mode of passion result in distress, and actions performed in the mode of ignorance result in foolishness."

As we continue through life, we develop habits that may last for many years. This certainly has a great bearing on our mind and consciousness at the time of death. This is very important to understand, because when we die in a particular mode, as can be discerned by our thoughts and activities, we are thus given the immediate effect. "When one dies in the mode of goodness, he attains to the pure higher planets. When one dies in the mode of passion, he takes birth among those engaged in fruitive activities; and when one dies in the mode of ignorance, he takes birth in the animal kingdom. (*Bg*.14.14-15). . . Those situated in the mode of goodness gradually go upward to the higher planets; those in the mode of passion live on the earthly planets; and those in the mode of ignorance go down to the hellish worlds." (*Bg*.14.18)

"Made to wander as the reaction of his fruitive work, the conditioned soul, by contact with the mode of goodness, takes birth among the sages or demigods. By contact with the mode of passion he becomes a demon or human being, and by association with the mode of ignorance he takes birth as a ghost or in the animal kingdom. Just as one may imitate persons whom one sees dancing and singing, similarly the soul, although never the doer of material activities, becomes captivated by material intelligence and is thus forced to imitate its qualities." (*Bhag*.11.22.52-53)

The *Manu-samhita* gives more specific information on the destination of one who dies in any of the material modes.

"But know this threefold course of transmigration that depends on the three qualities to be again threefold; low, middling, and high, according to the particular nature of the acts and of the knowledge of each person. Immovable beings [such as plants], insects both great and small, fishes, snakes, tortoises, cattle, and wild animals, are the lowest conditions to which the quality of Darkness [tamo-guna] heads. Elephants, horses, shudras, and despicable barbarians, lions, tigers, and boars are the middling states caused by the quality of Darkness. Charanas, Suparnas [a class of great birds], and hypocrites, Rakshashas [demons who eat human flesh and can assume many forms] and Pishacas [evil demons who are often invisible and can possess people] belong to the highest rank of conditions among those produced by Darkness.

"Ghallas, mallas [wrestlers and jesters], natas [actors], men who subsist by despicable occupations, and those addicted to gambling and drinking form the lowest order of conditions caused by Activity (passion or raja-guna). Kings and kshatriyas [warriors], the domestic priests of kings, and those who delight in the warfare of disputations constitute the middling rank of the states caused by the mode of Activity. The Gandharvas [angel-like beings], the Guhyakas [spirits with luminous bodies who exercise their powers from secret places], and the servants of the gods, likewise the Apsaras [heavenly dancing girls], belong to the highest rank of conditions produced by Activity." (Manu.12.41-47)

"Hermits, ascetics, brahmanas, the crowds of the Vaimanika deities [those who move in the air on their chariots], the lunar mansions, and the Daityas [the giants who were descendants of Diti] form the first and lowest rank of the existences caused by Goodness (sattva-guna). Sacrificers, the sages, the gods, the [personified] Vedas, the heavenly lights, the years, the manes [ancestors], and the Sadhyas [semi-divine celestial beings or intermediate gods], constitute the second order of existences caused by Goodness. The sages declare Brahma, the creators of the universe, the law, the Great One [Supreme Lord], and the Undiscernible One [Paramatma or Supersoul] to constitute the highest order of beings produced by Goodness. Thus, the result of the threefold action, the whole system of transmigration which consists of three classes, each with three subdivisions, and which includes all created beings, has been fully pointed out." (*Manu*.12.48-51)

Of course, this description is not complete in detailing all the various species of life within the universe or the conditions one attains as a result of associating with particular material modes. However, one can definitely see that living entities will raise or lower themselves according to their involvement with the modes of nature. This is made clear in *Srimad-Bhagavatam* (11.25.21-22): "Learned persons dedicated to Vedic culture are elevated by the mode of goodness to higher and higher positions. The mode of ignorance, on the other hand, forces one to fall headfirst into lower and lower births. And by the mode of passion one continues transmigrating through human bodies. Those who leave this world in the mode of goodness go to the heavenly planets, those who pass away in the mode of passion remain in the world of human beings, and those dying in the mode of ignorance must go to hell. But those who are free from the influence of all modes of nature come to Me [the Supreme in the spiritual abode]."

This is the goal of the varnashrama system, to gradually elevate anyone to higher and higher levels of consciousness, regardless of what level they may be on at present. This is going from being a Brahmachari or student, to Grihastha or married life, to Vanaprastha or retired life with a bent toward spiritual progress, and then to Sannyasa, which is dedication to spiritual advancement and withdrawal from material affairs and worldly activities. That way, by the time we attain old age and are ready to leave this world, and by proper faith and pious activities, we can attain a level of consciousness that is as spiritual as possible that will help propel us into the spiritual realm after death.

As long as we are engaged in activities or involved with ideas that are affected by any of the modes of material nature, we will continually transmigrate from one situation to another within this enclosed, cosmic creation. It is similar to a penitentiary or correctional facility. We may be locked up in a big jail cell or a small cell, one with a television or without, or serve as a cook or in making license plates, as some prisons make the inmates do. But whatever the case, we are still in jail. Likewise, as long as we remain influenced by the modes of material nature, we will never experience the freedom outside the material energy. We will always be forced to accept the good or bad results given to us by our karma according to the modes with which we associate.

BECOMING FREE FROM THE MODES

Reaching the spiritual realm also means becoming free from the modes of material nature, the *gunas*, and raising above material consciousness. So how do we do that?

First of all, by recognizing which modes are affecting us from the qualities of our acts and thoughts, as previously described, we can understand what kind of future life we are creating for ourselves. And by understanding the law of karma, we can know what sort of reactions we may enjoy or suffer. Therefore, it becomes obvious how important it is to learn the process of becoming free from the modes of material nature, which, if a person follows the process of varnashrama, will help accomplish this.

The advantage of becoming free from the material modes is explained in *Bhagavad-gita*: "When the embodied being is able to transcend these three modes, he can become free from birth, death, old age and their distresses and can enjoy nectar even in this life." (*Bg.*14.20)

Being born, working hard for so many things, only to grow old, diseased, and finally die is certainly not something to which we happily look forward. So, who would not be interested in learning a way to avoid these unwanted miseries? According to *Bhagavad-gita*, there certainly is a way to be free from these distresses, and the process is to transcend the modes. So, how do we do this?

This question was also asked by Arjuna five thousand years ago to Lord Krishna. "Arjuna inquired: 'O my dear Lord, by what symptoms is one known who is transcendental to those modes? What is his behavior? And how does he transcend the modes of nature?' The Blessed Lord said: 'He who does not hate illumination, attachment and delusion when they are present, nor longs for them when they disappear; who is seated like one unconcerned, being situated beyond these material reactions of the modes of nature, who remains firm, knowing that the modes alone are active; who regards alike pleasure and pain, and looks on a clod, a stone, and a piece of gold with an equal eye; who is wise and holds praise and blame to be the same; who is unchanged in honor and dishonor, who treats friend and foe alike, who has abandoned all fruitive undertakings--such a man is said to have transcended the modes of nature. One who engages in full devotional service, who does not fall down in any circumstance, at once transcends the modes of material nature and thus comes to the level of Brahman.'" (*Bg*.14.21-26)

Actually, in the human species of life, it is our duty to become free of the material modes because only in this human form do we have the ability to do so. "Therefore, having achieved this human form of life, which allows one to develop full knowledge, those who are intelligent should free themselves from all contamination of the modes of nature and engage exclusively in loving service to Me [Lord Krishna]." (*Bhag*.11.25.33)

Getting free from the modes is a scientific process that is meant for everyone. The system for arranging society, according to the Vedic literature, is to provide the facility for all people to elevate themselves from whatever their situation is to a higher level of existence. This means raising oneself from the mode of ignorance or passion to at least the mode of goodness. "One must conquer the modes of passion and ignorance by developing the mode of goodness, and then one must become detached from the mode of goodness, by promoting oneself to the platform of *sudha sattva* [the transcendental platform of pure goodness]. All this can be automatically done if one engages in the service of the spiritual master with faith and devotion. In this way, one can conquer the influence of the modes of nature." (*Bhag*.7.15.25)

In the mode of goodness, one can begin to understand spiritual knowledge very easily. But in our search for spiritual progress, we must have a teacher or spiritual master to guide us and give us transcendental knowledge. By accepting such guidance from a bonafide and pure spiritual representative, one can swiftly conquer the modes of nature, even the mode of material goodness, and reach pure goodness, the transcendental, spiritual atmosphere.

In this way, by the practice of yoga and following the instruction of the genuine spiritual master, one may remain aloof from material activities by being fixed on the spiritual platform. Thus, one avoids acting within the modes. "A person fixed in transcendental knowledge is freed from conditioned life by giving up his false identification with the products of the material modes of nature. Seeing these products as simply illusion, he avoids entanglement with the modes of nature, although constantly among them. Because the modes of nature and their products are simply not real, he does not accept them." (*Bhag*.11.26.2)

So, by being fixed in spiritual consciousness, one no longer transmigrates after death to the destinations acquired by those who are influenced by the modes of nature. Lord Krishna explains this as follows: "O gentle Uddhava, all these different phases of conditioned life arise from work born of the modes of material nature. The living entity who conquers these modes, manifested from the mind, can dedicate himself to Me by the process of devotional service [bhakti-yoga] and, thus, attain pure love for Me." (*Bhag*.11.25.32)

"As soon as irrevocable loving service is established in the heart, the effects of nature's modes of passion and ignorance, such as lust, desire and hankering, disappear from the heart. Then the devotee is established in goodness, and he becomes completely happy." (*Bhag*.1.2.19)

Once we are free from the modes, we will be able to engage in our natural, spiritual activities. This is the kind of freedom for which we are always hankering. We never like to be detained or limited in our pursuits for happiness, but in material life we experience all kinds of problems or responsibilities with which we do not necessarily want to deal. Therefore, Sri Krishna explains that, "A wise sage, free from all material association and unbewildered, should subdue his senses and worship Me. He should conquer the modes of passion and ignorance by engaging himself only with things in the mode of goodness. Then, being fixed in devotional service, the sage should also conquer the material mode of goodness by indifference toward the modes. Thus pacified within his mind, the spirit soul, freed from the modes of nature, gives up the very cause of his conditional life and attains Me." (*Bhag*.11.25.34-35)

Of course, there may be those who do not agree with this analysis, but their disagreements are simply further proof of their interaction with the modes of nature. For example, there may be philosophers and scientists who try to understand how things go on in this world. But as long as they are controlled by the modes of nature or the universal laws, they will never get a clear understanding of how they work. It is like trying to analyze the cause of a fire while being blinded by the smoke. You must first be free from the smoke to see the fire clearly. That is why Lord Krishna explains, "When philosophers argue, 'I don't choose to analyze this particular case in the same way as you have,' it is simply My own insurmountable energies [the modes] that are motivating their analytic disagreements. By interaction of My energies different opinions arise. But for those who have fixed their intelligence in Me, controlling the senses, differences of perception disappear, and consequently the very cause for argument is removed." (*Bhag*.11.22.5-6)

Once the dualities in material vision, caused by the modes of nature, are removed, the Absolute Truth can be perceived, and by experiencing the Absolute, all reasons for argument are eliminated. Thus, one can understand what reality is and be completely satisfied within himself. The process of devotional service, bhakti-yoga, to the Supreme Lord has been described as the process which removes the influence of the modes of nature and which invites the Lord to reveal Himself to the living entity. This state of perfection is described by Lord Krishna in *Srimad-Bhagavatam* (11.25.36): "Freed from the subtle conditioning of the mind and from the modes of nature born of material consciousness, the living entity becomes completely satisfied by experiencing My transcendental form. He no longer searches for enjoyment in the external [temporary material] energy, nor does he contemplate or remember such enjoyment within himself."

This, therefore, is real freedom from the modes of material nature by which one is able to be released from further entrapment in karma and the cycle of repeated births and deaths. This is also the perfectional stage of following the Vedic system of varna and ashramas while following the means for spiritual development, such as bhakti-yoga. This is how the system of varnashrama can benefit everyone in all of society, well over and above the materialistic caste system that we find today. This is also why the present caste system should be avoided or given up, while distinguishing the difference and importance of the truly Vedic system of varna and ashramas.

APPENDIX

Gotras: A Simple Explanation

Since gotras were mentioned earlier, it is best to give this a deeper explanation. The reason is that this also shows our individual connection to the Vedic lineages going back to ancient times.

Whenever you go to visit a temple in India, and participate in the doing pujas or rituals, the priest will often ask you to which gotra your family line belongs. Then you tell him your gotra, and usually the names of your father and mother, and he puts that into the recitation of prayers to offer to the deity you are worshiping, and to get blessings from that deity. In other cases, a person introduces himself to elders by stating one's name and gotra. This is a form of acknowledging one's ancestral ties and all that has been given by one's ancestors.

How the system of gotra works can be explained like this. First of all, the original spiritual knowledge was given by the Supreme Being to Lord Brahma, the secondary creator of the universe. From Brahma came the powerful rishis who were capable of receiving this knowledge and preserving it, and then spreading it throughout the universe, and down through the generations of humanity.

So, after the universal creation under the guidance of Lord Brahma, it is recorded that he had 27 sons who were also progenitors for mankind, called Prajapatis, who were the seeds of humanity which spread throughout the world. The familial line from each of these Prajapatis is called a gotra. So the names of the gotra carries the name of each one of these sages. In this way, the 27 sons of Brahma were also the beginnings for the 27 gotras.

These sons of Brahma were also learned sages called rishis. These seers came to be known as the *mantra-drishtaraha*, seers of the Vedic mantras. The main seven sages, called the Saptarshis (Seven Rishis), are Kashyapa, Vashistha, Bharadwaj, Kapila, Atri, Vishvamitra, and Gautama. It is also these Saptarshis which help preserve and propagate spiritual knowledge to humanity for everyone's benefit. Additional sons of Brahma include Svayambhuva Manu, Adharma, Praheti, Heti, Aristanemi, Bhrigu, Daksha, Pracetas, Sthanu, Samshraya, Sesha, Vikrita, Kardama, Kratu, Pulaha, Pulastya, and Agiras, along with Marichi, Bhrigu, and Agastya.

The gotra also helps establish your identity as part of the Vedic tradition, and that your family lineage can be traced back to one of the original great rishis or sages from whom the knowledge of Vedic culture has descended. We all belong to one of these gotras, whether we know them or not. But it is a great insight to know your gotra. Yet it is no great loss if you do not.

However, these gotras have since increased through time to include many others. There are now two hundred and forty-nine gotras, of which approximately forty are common today. Of these forty include: Vatula, Atreya, Garga, Kaundinnya, Kaushika, Gautama, Naidhruva-kashyapa, Harita, Bharadvaja, Shandilya, Maudgalya, and Shrivasta.

Gotras are further classified into five groups, depending upon the number of rishi descendants in a particular gotra. These groups are:

1. Ekarsheya-pravara-gotra, having one rishi descendant.
2. Dvayarsheya-pravara-gotra, having two rishi descendants.
3. Treyarsheya-pravara-gotra, having three rishi descendants.

4. Pancharisheya-pravara-gotra, having five rishi descendants.
5. Saptarisheya-pravara-gotra, having seven rishi descendants.

One example could be a Treyarsheya-pravara-gotra of Vatula, Atreya, and Kaushika gotras, or another line of three (treya) rishis.

Another point about this is that in India, one's gotra is important because they help avoid what would be called inbreeding, or families marrying within their own gotra. In fact, sometimes they avoid four gotras, including your father's gotra, your mother's, your paternal grandmother's, and your maternal grandmother's. Marrying someone outside of these four mentioned gotras is said to help prevent birth defects or deformities in their children by keeping people from marrying within the same genetic roots.

In any case, this is a Vedic tradition that seems to be traced back to the beginning of time.

GLOSSARY

Acarya--the spiritual master who sets the proper standard by his own example.

Ahankara--false ego, identification with matter.

Ahimsa--nonviolence.

Ananda--spiritual bliss.

Ananta--unlimited.

Aranyaka--sacred writings that are supposed to frame the essence of the *Upanishads*.

Arati--the ceremony of worship when incense and ghee lamps are offered to the Deities.

Arca-vigraha--the worshipable Deity form of the Lord made of stone, wood, etc.

Artha--the aspect of life for working to earn a living and make money.

Aryan--a noble person, one who is on the Vedic path of spiritual advancement.

Asana--postures for meditation, or exercises for developing the body into a fit instrument for spiritual advancement.

Asat--that which is temporary.

Ashrama--one of the four orders of spiritual life, such as *brahmacari* (celibate student), *grihastha* (married householder), *vanaprastha* (retired stage), and *sannyasa* (renunciate); or the abode of a spiritual teacher or *sadhu*.

Atma--the self or soul. Sometimes means the body, mind, and senses.

Atman--usually referred to as the Supreme Self.

Avatara--an incarnation of the Lord who descends from the spiritual world.

Avidya--ignorance or nescience.

Aum--*om* or *pranava*

Bhagavan--one who possesses all opulences, God.

Bhajan--song of worship.

Bhakta--a devotee of the Lord who is engaged in *bhakti-yoga*.

Bhakti--love and devotion for God.

Bhakti-yoga--the path of offering pure devotional service to the Supreme.

Brahma--the demigod of creation who was born from Lord Vishnu, the first created living being and the engineer of the secondary stage of creation of the universe when all the living entities were manifested.

Brahmachari–The first of the ashramas in the Vedic social arrangement. This indicates one being a student, generally celebate, and can include ages 5 to 25 years old.

Brahmajyoti--the great white light or effulgence which emanates from the body of the Lord.

Brahmaloka--the highest planet or plane of existence in the universe; the planet where Lord Brahma lives.

Brahman--the spiritual energy; the all-pervading impersonal aspect of the Lord; or the Supreme Lord Himself.

Brahmana or brahmin--one of the four orders of society; the intellectual class of men who have been trained in the knowledge of the *Vedas* and initiated by a spiritual master.

Brahmana--the supplemental books of the four primary *Vedas*. They usually contained instructions for performing Vedic *agnihotras*, chanting the *mantras*, the purpose of the rituals, etc. The *Aitareya* and *Kaushitaki Brahmanas* belong to the *Rig-veda*, the *Satapatha Brahmana* belongs to the *White Yajur-veda*, and the *Taittiriya Brahmana* belongs to the *Black Yajur-veda*. The *Praudha* and *Shadvinsa Brahmanas* are two of the eight *Brahmanas* belonging to the *Atharva-veda*.

Caste–The name of a class in the social arrangement, but based primarily on one's birth rather than one's qualifications and abilities or intellectual development. The perverted form of Varna and Varnashrama.

Casteism–The system of determining one's social status based on one's birth. The perverted form of the Vedic system of Varnashrama.

Deity--the *arca-vigraha*, or worshipful form of the Divinity in the temple.

Deva–a demigod, or higher being.

Devaloka--the higher planets or planes of existence of the devas.

Dharma--the essential nature and duty of the living being.

Dualism--as related in this book, it refers to the Supreme as both an impersonal force (Brahman) as well as the Supreme Person.

Dwaita--dualism, the principle that the Absolute Truth consists of the infinite Supreme Being along with the infinitesimal, individual souls.

Gayatri--the spiritual vibration or *mantra* from which the other *Vedas* were expanded and which is chanted by those who are initiated as *brahmanas* and given the spiritual understanding of Vedic philosophy.

Goloka Vrindavana--the name of Lord Krishna's spiritual planet.

Gosvami--one who is master of the senses.

Gotra–the lineage in which a person is born that can be traced back to one of the great Vedic sages.

Grihastha–The householder and married stage of life. Grihastha means married life with the pursuit of spiritual advancement, while Grihamedhi means householder life for material pleasure, as much eating, sleeping, and mating as possible.

Gunas--the modes of material nature of which there is
    sattva (goodness), *rajas* (passion), and *tamas*
    (ignorance).
Guru--a spiritual master.
Harinam--refers to the name of the Lord, Hari.
Hatha-yoga--a part of the yoga system which stresses
    various sitting postures and exercises.
Jati–One's birth and family situation.
Japa--the chanting one performs, usually softly, for one's
    own meditation.
Jiva--the individual soul or living being.
Jivanmukta--a liberated soul, though still in the material
    body and universe.
Jiva-shakti--the living force.
Jnana--knowledge which may be material or spiritual.
Jnana-yoga--the process of linking with the Supreme
    through empirical knowledge and mental
    speculation.
Kali--the demigoddess who is the fierce form of the wife of
    Lord Shiva. The word   *kali* comes from *kala*,
    the Sanskrit word for time: the power that dissolves
    or destroys everything.
Kali-yuga--the fourth and present age, the age of quarrel
    and confusion, which lasts 432,000 years and began
    5,000 years ago.
Kalki--future incarnation of Lord Vishnu who appears at
    the end of Kali-yuga.
Kalpa--a day in the life of Lord Brahma which lasts a
    thousand cycles of the four   *yugas*.
Kama–the goal of seeking pleasure, one of the aspects for
    fulfilling one's desires.
Karma--material actions performed in regard to developing
    one's position or for future results which produce
    karmic reactions. It is also the reactions one endures
    from such fruitive activities.

Karma-yoga--system of yoga for using one's activities for spiritual advancement.

Kirtana--chanting or singing the glories of the Lord.

Krishna--the name of the original Supreme Personality of Godhead which means the most attractive and greatest pleasure. He is the source of all other incarnations, such as Vishnu, Rama, Narasimha, Narayana, Buddha, Parashurama, Vamanadeva, Kalki at the end of Kali-yuga, etc.

Krishnaloka--the spiritual planet where Lord Krishna resides.

Kshatriya--the second class of *varna* of society, or occupation of administrative or protective service, such as warrior or military personel.

Mahabharata--the great epic of the Pandavas, which includes the *Bhagavad-gita*, by Vyasadeva.

Maha-mantra--the best *mantra* for self-realization in this age, called the Hare Krishna *mantra*.

Maha-Vishnu or Karanodakasayi Vishnu--the Vishnu expansion of Lord Krishna from whom all the material universes emanate.

Mandir--a temple.

Mantra--a sound vibration which prepares the mind for spiritual realization and delivers the mind from material inclinations. In some cases a *mantra* is chanted for specific material benefits.

Maya--illusion, or anything that appears to not be connected with the eternal Absolute Truth.

Mayavadi--the impersonalist or voidist who believes that the Supreme has no form, or that any form of God is but a product of *maya*.

Moksha--liberation from material existence.

Murti--a Deity of the Lord or an image of a demigod or spiritual master that is worshiped.

Narayana--the four-handed form of the Supreme Lord.

Nirguna--without material qualities.

Nirvana--the state of no material miseries, usually the goal
    of the Buddhists or voidists.

Om or *Omkara--pranava*, the transcendental *om mantra*,
    generally referring to the attributeless or impersonal
    aspects of the Absolute.

Prana--the life air or cosmic energy.

Pranayama--control of the breathing process as in *astanga*
or *raja-yoga*.

Prasada--food or other articles that have been offered to
    the Deity in the temple and then distributed amongst
    people as the blessings or mercy of the Deity.

Puja--the worship offered to the Deity.

Pujari--the priest who performs worship, *puja*, to the Deity.

Ramayana--the great epic of the incarnation of Lord
    Ramachandra.

Sadhana--a specific practice or discipline for attaining God
    realization.

Samsara--rounds of life; cycles of birth and death;
    reincarnation.

Sanatana-dharma--the eternal nature of the living being, to
    love and render service to the supreme lovable
    object, the Lord.

Sannyassa–The renounced order of life when a person gives
    up married life and accepts a purely spiritual
    lifestyle to attain the perfection of life.

Satya-yuga--the first of the four ages which lasts 1,728,000
    years.

Shastra--the authentic revealed Vedic scripture.

Shiva--the benevolent one, the demigod who is in charge of
    the material mode of ignorance and the destruction
    of the universe. Part of the triad of Brahma, Vishnu,
    and Shiva who continually create, maintain, and
    destroy the universe. He is known as Rudra when
    displaying his destructive aspect.

Shudra–The working or laborer class of the Varnashrama
social arrangement. Includes poets, writers,
musicians, craftsmen, etc.

Srimad-Bhagavatam--the most ripened fruit of the tree of
Vedic knowledge compiled by Vyasadeva.

Sruti--scriptures that were received directly from God and
transmitted orally by *brahmanas* or *rishis* down
through succeeding generations. Traditionally, it is
considered the four primary *Vedas*.

Treta-yuga--the second of the four ages which lasts
1,296,000 years.

Upanishads--the portions of the *Vedas* which primarily
explain philosophically the Absolute Truth. It is
knowledge of Brahman which releases one from the
world and allows one to attain self-realization when
received from a qualified teacher. Except for the *Isa
Upanishad*, which is the 40th chapter of the
Vajasaneyi Samhita of the *Sukla Vedanta-
sutras*--the philosophical conclusion of the four
Vedas.

Vaishya–The merchant, farming and banking class of the
Varnashrama system.

Vanaprastha–The retired stage of life when a couple gives
up their occupations and preferably begins to
prepare for a more spiritual mode of lifestyle.

Varna–The name of the sections of the Vedic social
arrangement, which includes the Brahmana,
Kshatriya, Vaishya and Shudra.

Varnashrama–The Vedic system of social arrangement so
everyone can engage in a way for social harmony,
and a part of the universal form of the Lord.

Vedas--generally means the four primary *samhitas; Rig,
Yajur, Sama, Atharva.*

Vishnu--the expansion of Lord Krishna who enters into the
material energy to create and maintain the cosmic
world.

Vrindavana--the place where Lord Krishna displayed His
      village pastimes 5,000 years ago, and is considered
      to be part of the spiritual abode.

Vyasadeva--the incarnation of God who appeared as the
      greatest philosopher who compiled the main
      portions of the Vedic literature into written form.

REFERENCES

Bhagavad-gita As It Is, translated by A. C. Bhaktivedanta
    Swami, Bhaktivedanta Book Trust, New York/Los
    Angeles, 1972

Bhavisya Purana, by Srila Vyasadeva, translated by
    Bhumipati Dasa, published by Rasbikarilal & Sons,
    Vrindavana, India, 2007.

Hymns of the Rig-veda, tr. by Griffith, Motilal Banarsidass,
    Delhi, 1973

Mahabharata, Sanskrit Text With English Translations, by
    M. N. Dutt, Parimal Publications, Delhi, 2001

Skanda Purana, by Srila Vyasadeva, Purnaprajna Dasa,
    Rasbihari Lal & Sons, Vrindavana, India, 2005.

Shri Ramcharitmanas

Srimad-Bhagavatam, translated by A. C. Bhaktivedanta
    Swami, Bhaktivedanta Book trust, New York/Los
    Angeles, 1972

The Law of Manu, [*Manu-samhita*], translated by Georg
    Buhlerg, Motilal Banarsidass, Delhi, 1970

Vishnu Purana, translated by H. H. Wilson, Nag
    Publishers, Delhi

INDEX

ABOUT THE AUTHOR

Stephen Knapp grew up in a Christian family, during which time he seriously studied the Bible to understand its teachings. In his late teenage years, however, he sought answers to questions not easily explained in Christian theology. So he began to search through other religions and philosophies from around the world and started to find the answers for which he was looking. He also studied a variety of occult sciences, ancient mythology, mysticism, yoga, and the spiritual teachings of the East. After his first reading of the *Bhagavad-gita*, he felt he had found the last piece of the puzzle he had been putting together through all of his research. Therefore, he continued to study all of the major Vedic texts of India to gain a better understanding of the Vedic science.

It is known amongst all Eastern mystics that anyone, regardless of qualifications, academic or otherwise, who does not engage in the spiritual practices described in the Vedic texts cannot actually enter into understanding the depths of the Vedic spiritual science, nor acquire the realizations that should accompany it. So, rather than pursuing his research in an academic atmosphere at a university, Stephen directly engaged in the spiritual disciplines that have been recommended for hundreds of years. He continued his study of Vedic knowledge and spiritual practice under the guidance of a spiritual master. Through this process, and with the sanction of His Divine Grace A. C. Bhaktivedanta Swami Prabhupada, he became initiated into the genuine and authorized spiritual line of the Brahma-Madhava-Gaudiya *sampradaya*, which is a disciplic succession that descends back through Sri Caitanya Mahaprabhu and Sri Vyasadeva, the compiler of Vedic literature, and further back to Sri Krishna. At that time he was given the spiritual name of Sri Nandanandana dasa. In this way, he has been practicing yoga, especially bhakti-yoga, for forty plus years, and has attained many insights and realizations through this means. Besides being *brahminically* initiated, Stephen has also been to India several times and traveled extensively throughout the country, visiting most of the major holy places and gaining a wide variety of spiritual experiences that only such places can give. He has also spent nearly 40 years in the management of various temples.

Stephen has put the culmination of over forty years of continuous research and travel experience into his books in an effort to share it with those who are also looking for spiritual understanding. More books are forthcoming, so stay in touch through his website to find out further developments.

More information about Stephen, his projects, books, free ebooks, and numerous articles and videos can be found on his website at: www.stephen-knapp.com   or http://stephenknapp.info   or his blog at http://stephenknapp.wordpress.com.

Stephen has continued to write books that include in
The Eastern Answers ot the Mysteries of Life series:
The Secret Teachings of the Vedas;
The Universal Path to Enlightenment;
The Vedic Prophecies: A New Look into the Future;
How the Universe was Created and Our Purpose In It.
He has also written:
Toward World Peace: Seeing the Unity Between Us All;
Facing Death: Welcoming the Afterlife;
The Key to Real Happiness;
Proof of Vedic Culture's Global Existence;
Vedic Culture: The Difference It Can Make In Your Life;
Reincarnation and Karma: How They Really Affect Us;
Power of the Dharma: An Introduction to Hinduism and Vedic Culture;
The Eleventh Commandment: The Next Step in Social Spiritual Development;

The Heart of Hinduism: The Eastern Path to Freedom, Empowerment and Illumination;
Seeing Spiritual India: A Guide to Temples, Holy Sites, Festivals and Traditions;
Crimes Against India: And the Need to Protect its Vedic Tradition;
Yoga and Meditation: Its Real Purpose and How to Get Started;
Avatars, Gods and Goddesses of the Vedic Tradition;
The Soul: Understanding Our Real Identity;
Prayers, Mantras and Gayatris: A Collection for Insight, Protection, Spiritual Growth, and Many Other Blessings;
Krishna Deities and Their Miracles: How the Images of Lord Krishna Interact With Their Devotees;
Defending Vedic Dharma: Tackling the Issues to Make a Difference;
Mysteries of the Ancient Vedic Empire,
and
Destined for Infinity, an exciting novel for those who prefer lighter reading, or learning spiritual knowledge in the context of an action oriented, spiritual adventure.

More books and articles are always in the making, so stay tuned for whatever may develop next.

www.Stephen-Knapp.com
http://stephenknapp.info

Be sure to visit Stephen's web site. It provides lots of information on many spiritual aspects of Vedic and spiritual philosophy, and Indian culture for both beginners and the scholarly. You will find:

1. All the descriptions and contents of Stephen's books, how to order them, and keep up with any new books or articles that he has written.
2. Reviews and unsolicited letters from readers who have expressed their appreciation for his books, as well as his website.
3. Free online booklets are also available for your use or distribution on meditation, why be a Hindu, how to start yoga, meditation, etc.
4. Helpful prayers, mantras, gayatris, and devotional songs.
5. Over a hundred enlightening articles that can help answer many questions about life, the process of spiritual development, the basics of the Vedic path, or how to broaden our spiritual awareness. Many of these are emailed among friends or posted on other web sites.
6. Over 150 color photos taken by Stephen during his travels through India. There are also descriptions and 40 photos of the huge and amazing Kumbha Mela festival.
7. Directories of many Krishna and Hindu temples around the world to help you locate one near you, where you can continue your experience along the Eastern path.
8. Postings of the recent archeological discoveries that confirm the Vedic version of history.
9. Photographic exhibit of the Vedic influence in the Taj Mahal, questioning whether it was built by Shah Jahan or a pre-existing Vedic building.
10. A large list of links to additional websites to help you continue your exploration of Eastern philosophy, or provide more information and news about India, Hinduism, ancient Vedic culture, Vaishnavism, Hare Krishna sites, travel, visas, catalogs for books and paraphernalia, holy places, etc.

11. A large resource for vegetarian recipes, information on its benefits, how to get started, ethnic stores, or non-meat ingredients and supplies.
12. A large "Krishna Darshan Art Gallery" of photos and prints of Krishna and Vedic divinities. You can also find a large collection of previously unpublished photos of His Divine Grace A. C. Bhaktivedanta Swami.

This site is made as a practical resource for your use and is continually being updated and expanded with more articles, resources, and information. Be sure to check it out.

Made in the USA
Middletown, DE
08 December 2017